Dark Side of Genius

"Death opens a door out of a little, dark room (that's all the life we have known before it) into a great, real place where the true sun shines and we shall meet."

— C.S. Lewis, Till We Have Faces

"Holy places are dark places. It is life and strength, not knowledge and words, that we get in them. Holy wisdom is not clear and thin like water, but thick and dark like blood."

— C.S. Lewis, Till We Have Faces

Poetry Collection of Lucian Wilde

All rights are reserved.

No part of this publication may be reproduced, stored in a retrieval system or transmitted in any form or by any means, electronic, mechanical, photocopying, recording or otherwise, without prior permission of author or Stonelight Publishing.

READERS SPEAK OUT

(Lucian's Poetry)

Something wicked sweet this way comes! Out of the dark ages we received Poe. Now we have Lucian Wilde! This book is a must have for any and all lovers of the dark poetry and romantic mystery. You'll never want to put it down. I can't wait for his other book "Lost Vampire Letters" and The Novel "Secret of the Blood"

------Chandra Kolobus Lynch

I recommend Blood Magic Stir wholeheartedly. It's beautifully written and very compelling. Lucian is a wonderful writer and once "Bitten" by him you will never be the same!

-------Loretta Kirtman Terry

The poetry of vampire character Lucian Wilde is captivating, romantic, and visual. There are not that many writers who can captivate me with just their poetry, but LW manages to make me feel like I am being swept away on his words alone. Beautiful!!

-------Laura M. McCormick

Being well aware of the writings of Lucian Wilde, a fictional vampire poet, I started and finished this book the day it was delivered to my door. I wasn't disappointed in the slightest. It took me away to another place.....It made me feel as if I were to take my eyes off the book and look up, I would be surrounded by velvet and candles in a dark gothic castle, drinking wine and reading in another era of time. I am looking forward to the accompanying novel that goes along with this dark, poetic book.

   -------Ms. Claudette N. Saifert

I love to read the raw poems of Lucian Wilde. I sit with my cup of tea and open the book, just as the sun is about to go down, the shadowy light sets the mood for my bloody romance...

   ----Ashley

Lucian manages to bring a wonderful story to life.

Mystery, excitement, adventure and so much more rolled into one.

> ---- Raven EverNight

You are a fabulous visionary.

> --- Bebe Wahlstad

I feel happiness when I read your dark words and watch in wonder as you pursue and harass them with your mental clarity. It is as if you had devoured the whole World in your Imagination.

> --- Christina Yexley

TABLE OF CONTENTS

Poetry Tour 10

Devil's Love Letters...... 33

Blood Magic Stir.......... 49

Dark Side of Genius........156

Lucian's Short Journal Entrees

7 days... 7,27,79,114,126,142,188

The Haunted Piano ……..167

Red Chair in the Forest...189
(Earth's First Love)

Short Stories

The Ling Low………...…191
End of Illusion..…....….…206

Day 1

I shouldn't be writing these words. Words have become broken promises. My dearest Lilith, what have I become? Can you hear the sorrow in my voice and my tears of regret as I write you these clumsy words? I can't help myself, my sweet Lilith; you are love wrapped in a frail body of beauty that I only wish to hold forever. It is my only wish. I wanted the sun to stop shinning, but the light was only trying to help me to see…..I wanted the moon to be my only light, but it wasn't bright enough; my eyes cold, it wasn't as bright as yours. I'm stuck in your presence, in the absence of your kiss. I hate just thoughts, pictures, imagination; my soul cursed by them! If you can hear my voice, through the wind whispering through trees;

I'm giving you all my love…

Lonely Forest

The flat land is jealous of the hill, The hill is jealous of the mountain, The mountain is jealous of the sky, The sky is jealous of the wind , and the wind is jealous of the trees, and I'm jealous here without you...

Here in my lonely forest...

Mystic Woods at Night

Walking in the mystic woods, you see this man in the distance through the midnight fog. He's walking with a pack of wolves. You feel frightened, but can't stop wondering who he is? You begin to follow behind his shadow. The closer you get the more scared and attracted you become. Causing your heart to throb and pulsate throughout your lonely body. You get close enough to notice blood dripping from his hands. You become startled, terrified, and safe all in one breathless swallow. For some reason you feel, if you can only touch the blood of this mysterious man, you can heal him with your loving warmth. So you reach out to touch his hand from behind the tree, but then you find it is his hands that are healing you, from your own brokenness that has haunted you ever since you were a little girl. You've come out from the vines that had covered you with fear and with one glance of his passionate wild eyes, your fears disappear…

He looks at you and smiles and teaches you how to howl with the wolves, and He's not wearing a robe. He's wearing you. .He covers you with his warmth all over your chilled body... Every man that you ever thought loved you, vanished like the mist of yesterday's morning dew. The darkness is all around, and you're feeling the dark side of his dark sacred love. The kind of love that hangs God in the midnight, the kind of love that makes the wild wolf howls for its lost lover. The kind of love that makes the tiny little pond screams like an ocean. The pale moonlight smiles as you dance under the blood tree of forgiveness in the tattooed forest. Kissing your beautiful lips of death that brings you to life. How Gothic, How Romantic, How Immortal, How haunting is this dark side of love that whispers in the trees. Will you love me forever? "Yes my love" "Will you?" "Yes my love" "I always have...

Poetry Tour

A Thousand Deaths of Moonless Wolves

"Today I was so deep in the tattooed forest; she became my howling wind and my kiss of Blood…I could hardly see the sky with my hands raised in praise…The thunder was jealous, and the lighting struck me with blood shivers down my lips …Every branch, and twig seemed to capture me with a look…Staring at me when I buried my lost soul in a mirror of red… Like selling myself to the dirt of white shadows…I felt the screaming solitude…My spiritual water birth in the raining tears of dark love…My flesh all puddled up in its little grave ditch of Forever Lightless…Restless branches swaying winds of memories… Whispering your name…Picking the red rose…Drops of blood rolling down your hands from the cursed flower...Sleeping in the dust, like sleeping beauty…Waiting for me to kiss your lips once again…Story Changer, calling you Lilith…Hoping that I would never find my Eve again…Blocked by angels …Haunted by the Garden of Eden in the woods of Idaho…Sunshine dimmed by hovering leaves…My tired pale skin of peaches…Cold and lonely without your moonlight touch…My heart died a thousand deaths of moonless wolves… Today I was so deep in the tattooed forest; that you became my howling wind

My kiss of blood

Oh how I love you.

Your lovely round eyes

Oh how I need you

A thousand more times

Oh how I wonder

When you stole my heart

Oh How my soul takes a plunder

Without you… All is dark

Are you her? From my book

The woman every man wants to take a look

A millions flowers can't paint your soul

Every diamond in your presence becomes dull

If I could kiss every cell in your body

You make me alive… Into somebody

Oh… How I wish

My poetry tour… Worldwide kiss

If only to find… And taste your lips

A thousand words and thousand doors

Only you my lover… My poetry tour…….

One o'clock love

My Heart howls

Mirrors and Dark liquor

Veins… I sip within her

Sinking…Drinking…

In the Midnight blood

Your One o'clock love

Tell me the story

Of the dead in the night

White demons of snow

Angel wings let go

Where love first made

Where eyes first opened

Where I first saw you…

My one o'clock love

Holy Haunting

I've tried to escape

The invisible shape

The ghost & the cello

tears & pillows

God knows I've tried

Where love has died

Paranormal…sacred winds

Vampires… demons within

Dark Forest & dead end trails

Angelwolves and fiery hells

You know I've tried to escape

This invisible shape

Obsessions… Possessions

Riddle…Clues…Lessons

Drink this water and the thirst goes away

The unknown altar shows its face the other day

Unnerving sacred daunting

I've tried to escape…

This……. holy haunting…

Kiss in the Blue Dark

It doesn't matter who you are
I'll steal you away
With words you've never heard before
It doesn't matter who you are
I will steal you away
With those feelings you've never felt before

For you... I counted the stars
For you... I loved you far & far

Every night your wedding dress
Every night I give you my best

Melt you like the sun
Playing the moon just for fun

Kissing in the blue dark
Chasing wolves with wild hearts

Green Eyes on Ice

Kael Kael I keep seeing ur eyes

Kael Kael you're not meant to die

So round so green

You're my every dream

I can't break this ice

My soul died twice

That black dark wolf

Has brought this gulf

Between us… cold icy dust

I will kill him with my bare hands

If you can't see the moon

Neither will they

Please God… Don't take my green eyes away…

Green Eyes on Ice

Sexy Love of Heaven

This isn't sacrilegious… Oh Hear me

This isn't blasphemy… Oh Forgive me

Love me like King Solomon… Don't just tease me

This is more than naked…This is my soul

God hear me…This is my only soul

You promised us… We'd be higher than angels

You promised us a mansion

Sexy love of heaven.

Maker of romance

Where kisses were first made in the backwoods of heaven

You made love… You made us

I'm so tired of the world's dirty love

So tired of making ourselves gods

Kiss us to life again

Breathe us… to life again

Like holy lust… stare at me

Make me…Make me again

Sexy love of Heaven

Make me again…

Diamond Blue

Oh Delila… Oh Delila…

You make me come alive

With those brown charcoal eyes…

Oh Delila… Oh Delila…

Your soft Ivory skin…

Turning boys into sailors of men…

Oh Delila… Oh Delila…

If I tell my secret… I'll be so weak…

A taste of you… blue so sweet…

Oh Delila… Oh Delila…

Wars have been fought over you…

Oh thy beauty…Diamond blue…

Building a Soul

Build an empire and taste my beauty, she says

You'll die alone

Here's my shadow, you may touch it for free.

But it will cost you for my skin, a mansion indeed

Oh you poets love to pretend

Oh you romantics love to give in

Hammers and nails go build me a home

So I don't live in this world alone

"…I will…… I will…

After they've read my words on a thousand hills"

Oh she says… "It sounds like gold"

But the poet died in her shadow all alone

20 Years later she dies

Awoke with his poem in her hands and cries

So…. You don't want… not now

So we can't cry… somehow

The rose grows and thorns come alive

Pasted faces in the oceans we drown

Empty bottles…….. Drips of wine

I feel dead like all the dead before

I did build you a dream house with a red door

"Where" she said… "Where's my home?"

"Right here in my arms

You never died alone

When you left

I was building us our soul

In this place of forever……..

Now forever is our home……Building a Soul"

Dark Sun

There once was a dark sun

Who tried to be darker than everyone

Till the poet thought it was no longer fun

To be a light for the dark sun

He decided to leave her alone

Tired of being the dog's bone

Your colors have shown

Reap and sown

Such sadness… such sadness

The tortured artist sighs

Such sadness… such sadness

The poet says goodbye

Now the sun is bright

She is brighter than ever

But the moon has fallen

Fallen forever…

Wolves of Love

Still wild… Still wild…Love and still wild

Eyes still dark… Full of light

Sharp teeth… grace tasting night

New moon to be made…New earth to invade

New trees… new skies

New place where mortal never dies

Voices of glories…Sacred ghost stories

Angels in mountain rivers

Tales of old… demons shiver

Capture by the new moon

Wolves from above…Howling for love

Howling for love…

My Dark Love

My heart is black from all dungeons I've tried to clean

From the dark mirrors that just won't let me be

From all the one night loves that never satisfied me...

Oh my Dark Love

Some demons never go away

Though I try in all I pray

Make the moonlight sun of the day…

Oh my Dark Love

I'm thirsting for the sea

Cross of love that bleeds and bleeds

The breath of life….. I still need

My Dark Love

I've been a bad boy

Running around stealing grace and joy

Still looking for the right toy…

Oh my dark love

I need you…

You know how to make things white again…

Just one drop of holiness

Turn my heart red again

White sheets on a bed of pure

Oh dark love…I never meant to hurt her…

Poet of Earth

Nice trick walking on water

Poet of earth, sons and daughters

Nice trick… Nice Illusions

Nice love… Nice delusion

Turning water into wine

Teaching the sunlight how to shine

Nice one… calming the storms

Nice grip… twisting the devil's horns

Nice and thoughtful… To make us from above

Nice and truthful… To tell us that we're Loved

Nice and forgiving… When you offered life twice

If you believe… ……The dead shall come back to life

Poet of earth…. Makes us your poem tonight

Just Us, You, and the moonlight…

Oh Poet , poet of Earth

Howling Cross

Just in love with wicked night
    Eternal darkness forgotten light
        Sorry if I sound so impolite
            Unafraid of my blinded sight
                Sure you say you love me so

            When will you please just let me go
          Empty sacred phantom show
        Promise of hope and Lazarus is dead
        Truth keeps weeping inside my head

God's glory is on tour in the skies, God-craft on exhibit across the horizon. Madame Day holds classes every morning, Professor Night lectures each evening. Their words aren't heard, their voices aren't recorded, But their silence fills the earth: unspoken truth is spoken everywhere. God makes a huge dome for the sun - a superdome! The morning sun's a new husband leaping from his honeymoon bed, The daybreaking sun an athlete racing to the tape. That's how God's Word vaults across the skies from sunrise to sunset, Melting ice, scorching deserts, warming hearts to faith. The revelation of God is whole and pulls our lives together. The signposts of God are clear and point out the right road.
                ~ The Message

Day 2

I've heard it said that there is no greater love, when one lays down his life for his friend.

I never wanted to find out who said these perfect words; I wouldn't want to ruin such a great name by whoever quoted it, but now I want to know. Is It True!

Pale Dark Love

These waves have been too dark

An ocean without sight

I just want to open my eyes

Never say goodbye

I just want to live… In light

Bright shadows in white

Drown Me in Your Love

Stop these shaking hands

Shifting shadows shifting sands

Cry your tears from above

Drown me

Drown me

In your pale dark love

Pale Light

Running from the darkness into the night.

Hide my sins in the righteous moonlight

All these different demon stories

Hide and go seek in the Christ of glory

Oh give me this night, and hide this heart

Let me live your Mystic … Mysterious dark

The tattooed forest where poets recite

Strawberries of God & sacred delights

Dragon owls, wolves, & angel knights

Running from the darkness into the night

Where We Fall in love

In the Pale Light

3 drops of Love

You'll love me, you'll love me... in 3 drops of love
You'll you'll love me... in 11 drops of blood
You'll love me, you'll love me... My One o'clock love

Midnight moon and red sacred tea
Me and my lover sailing white shadowy seas
Phantoms of god in the Dark woods of house 123

Remember in the Tattooed Forest when you said,

"It makes me want to Bite...
Makes me want to fly... Deep into the night..."

You'll love me, you'll love me

In 11 drops of blood

You'll love me, you'll love me

My One O'clock love

You'll love me, you'll love me

3 drops of Love

Skin of Time Soul Forever

If we could live the notes of a piano
Feel the taste of forever
Hold ghost in the palms of out hands
Kiss like God is true
Love like Love is you
Skin of Time... Soul Forever
Fly our kites like hearts on clouds
Sleep in innocence ...Begin a new world
It's all unknown ..This could be my last poem
Skin of Time... Soul Forever
I'm tired of us not getting along
It's time for us to sing a new song
If blacks and whites could see
We are invisible inside of thee
Build a tree house in heaven's trees
Teach us how the birds believe
Skin of Time... Soul Forever
I'm crying... I'm dying
Death has killed us all
Our only enemy all along
I looked for a thousand ways
to get out of one way...
In this dark day
You scream never
Skin of Time... Soul Forever

Before the Trees Die

I wish to tell
This fairytale...
evolution is magic in slow motion
grace... hope... love's devotion.
a fairytale come true
The cross in love with you
I sit by this fire next to Jrr Tolkien
Warmth of mystic orange... let us soak in
Let me tell you before you sigh
Let me tell you before the trees die
"They can live to be hundreds of years old..."
Yes...that's what we wrote on our gravestones
Now you see... now you know why
We're all wind in the branches before the trees die...

Devil's Love Letters

"If Satan fell from heaven,
then what am I if I fell from hell..."

RUSHING IN MY VEINS

The touch of your hands

Rushing river
The kiss of your lips
Making me quiver
Wind through the trees
Pleading me insane
Rush of my blood
Rushing in my veins
I can feel in my soul's breath
The Reversing of death
Hurricanes…& Lover's games
My God rush & Heaven's flames
All rushing

LOVE & BE LOST

Staring at the moon
touching the old barn
Thinking of you
Causing no harm
walking down the old town
a thousand drunks without a sound
Is it too late to love and be lost
Like a river
Make me shiver
In this dark wishing well
Kiss and tell
take it off
All of it off
Love and be lost
Your skin
No sin
like in the beginning
God of no ending
Pink vase under the skirt
Happy tears In the dry desert
With bluish club lights
movie star spotlights
In your arms
In those old barns
Kiss me dumb
Kiss me young...
Love and Be Lost
Take it All off
Love and Be Lost

DEAD LOVE

If you cut the devil's eyes out, I wouldn't be in shock
And if you stole my heart, It would be in luck
Burn another tree in the fire
Watch it burn... burn away
I'll paint your eyes back with the ashes of my love
Fallen from the sky... The other sky above
Drink... Oh but Don't call me good
When lights go out... My night is forever
These violins & Those tears
My addiction & Those fears
White blood that bled and bled
Haunted by wings... Red and red
All over my black soul
Damned...
You Damned me away
Was I an angel...or your Dark prey
Where's heaven's glory
How I'm in the wrong story?
Ashes of my love
I've gone too far
Bring me back with your blood (1-J-1-7)
Bring me back from my dead love
My dead love
dead… dead...dead love…

GHOST LOVERS

Strawberry delight
My pink vase of light
the oceans calls us to the middle
deep past the sharks
past the sunken ship of the ark
Kissing your lips
In world of red
blood flower she said
We've become grace like thieves
gods of our every needs
All she wants is love
All she wants is a home
All she wants is to feel warm
All those lovers left cold
All those lovers false gold
No more ghost gods
No more coyote dogs
If I can only have
Just one real Love
In my covers
Disappear and be
ghost lovers...

BREATH TO DEATH

I wish I knew
Take these blues
I wish I knew
Where were you?
Does it matter now
I can feel it somehow
Does is matter now
"Nothing matters…"
My soul scatters
Death is playing with those I love
Death is a dark wicked dove
You say death is natural… I say not (1-C-15-26)
Watching love slowly rot…
I'm staring into the sunlight…
Knowing it's not right…
So I cry to the light…
&
Hide in the night…
Knowing it's not right…
Because Life brings Life to Life

MOON of LOVE

disappears like the night above
no one knows when the wind will blow…. (J-3-8)
Welcome to the light show
It will ALL be fine
Turning water into wine
So let me ask You
My dark of Blue.
Let me fly away like you do
and kiss her in the night
Death of twilight
High in the sky
Where angels are alive
I miss her lips, hips, and sips
Take my rib out with your holy pinch
Re-make what I've done wrong
Souls of a new song
Our mortal is fading gold
Yours is forever told
Lovers can make new skin....
We can't keep ours from growing old….
I love you...
……………………………..Story told...

Moon of Love (Story Told) Part 1

DARK POET DIE YOUNG (3)

Absinthe fills my soul
Lights begin to grow old
My eyes only see your face
Your lips are all I can taste
But instead of touching you
I run to the other side
To my fears with faithless tears
It's a pain that I can only feel
You don't think it's real?
God cries,
"Give this sickness a holy heart…"
In this darkness I belong
Where dark poets die young…

Dark Poets Die Young (#14)

the faster the candle burns
Higher the flames
The fallen angels falls
Charcoal soul stains
He was more than half a man
In these storms of dust and sinking sand…
Your voice sings with thunder
In this pile of mess we're under
In the light we can almost see
Like eyes of heaven cast on a dark tree
Such a beautiful melody
bitter sweet dark melancholy
He sung…
…………………….Dark Poets… Die young…

DARK PERCEPTION

I can only stay light for so long
I can only be right before wrong
Please let me fool you
Please let me school you
in my ways......................Dark days...
Licking dirty roads
Kissing your prince toad
Only to find my deception
My love is your dark perception...

HER LIPS ARE REAL

Dancing with tai chi
Secret life in me
Not your Inner self
Not on your book shelf
Long before words
Sounds never heard
In a time of no world
I was there thinking of you
The flower of blue
Flowers of red
Thoughts of skin
Veins that bled
I wanted to make you a tree for shade
I wanted to make you river to bathe
I fell in love you and what we made
I never stopped loving you
The phantom is me
Did you feel that?
Touch your lips
With your fingertips
I wanted to make touch
Just to see you blush
Did you feel that?
I'm taking out your bones
Wake up from your dream
It's not good to be alone
There she is…She's waiting…
Now you feel
Kiss her… Love her…
Her lips are real…

BUTTERFLY of the NIGHT

My black ghost smiles……. I smile back
My demons whisper……. I Whisper back
You wish you were here
In my light
In this delight
Strawberries of fun
Let's get naked in the sun
Oh Depression
I'm I your Obsession
Do I make you feel good
When I listen to your made up voice
To Capture me… To bleed me
If I say no, do you feel bad
Can you cry,,, and be a little sad
Here comes the black clouds
I laugh out loud
Weather is always for sure
The rain can wash us pure
I see Holy faces
In these dark places
Good night... To the day acting like night
You can't capture me in these dark porch lights
You can't have me
I'm a Butterfly of the night…
Floating away to heaven
To Heaven's light...

Lucian's Song of Songs # 13

JUST ME & MY BLUE FLOWER

I picked my blue flower
Watched her bleed red
Kissing your lips
Raised my heart from the dead
sunshine came from above
Forbidden secret love
kissing the clock away
Kiss me everyday
Unlimited hours
Oh sweet flower
Soft and new
My light my blue

Climbing heaven's tower...
Just Me & My Blue flower...

PINK SIPS
I taste your kiss
In front of the moon
Your Pale lips
…Burns
Your Pale love
…Stirs
Your Red lips
…Cures
Your Pink sips
…Turns
Down and around
Love and sounds
Comes like a soft hand
Like a hard fall
I fell
In your soul glue
Heaven inside you
I taste your sugar high
We make love and sounds
Like angels and clowns
Yes Yess Yesss
Love and sounds
Like angels and clowns

INVISBLE DOOR

Bright lips
Purple rain drips
You starve me for more
My Cinderella at the door
Take me in
Your secret mystery den

…………………………………….Ghost lover

Strawberry lips
Merry go round hips
Sugar high
Love sounds
………………………............. I drown

I fell from hell's north door
Right into heaven's west shores

This rush this holy kiss
God yes… I'll take this

Life's mistress no more
Gold hallways invisible Door

……………………………….In Your Invisible door

LOVE FIRST

Shouldn't love be first?
Yeah it can be worse
Death sounds better than hurt
Now I sound like the book of Job
Full of pain and no hope
Oh now I sound like the cross
Earth forgotten & lost
We're somewhere
I'm sure… right? Aren't we?
Roses full of thorns
All these devils with red horns
Come on Tell me!
Tell me the big surprise
Besides the heart of all wickedness
Besides the flesh filled with sickness
Is there more to life than scotch…
 darkness…love… & whores?
Is there more to life than all these bloody doors?
Love is my light…Darkness my confession
Give me resurrection… My holy obsession
I know… I know!
Shouldn't love be first!
I know… I know!
Love first!

SHADOWY PALE

Love what you do to me
I can't wait when it's just you and me
Like a kite... So high
Your love unties... Unblinds
I love what you do to me
Like a forest never walked in
Like a virgin all over again
You make me feel
You make me heal
The wolf howls all mysteries
Singing our bed lullaby
The pale gray stretches over your skin
Shadowy pale I live
In your rapids of love
Rapids of love
Shadowy pale I live
Shadowy Pale

Blood Magic Stir

Your blood my blood
Blood magic Stir

The Vampire and the Lonely Girl...

She wanted to feel the bite in the frost...What would it be like to be nailed to the cross...For years she lied in a filled lonely bed... For years her heart just bled instead...His was the other story...Fame, power and twisted glory...He wrote about the demon that became a part of him...A gothic slow fading dim...Like angels full of pride...Licking the sugar from their salty eyes...She tasted his blood and it tasted like scotch...She changed her mind about feeling like the cross...But once you've been nailed there's only one way down...The same one way to come back from the ground...Like the snake sniffing dusty cocaine...Like Frodo trying hard not to wear the ring...What happened to the prince, now that the princess is dead...What happened to the garden of Eden now that she has fled...You reap what you sow and sometimes it's forever...Like scars in God's hands, sometimes it's forever...Their just spinning and wandering in a lost world...He became the devil and she the lonely girl...One day they found each other...Right away they became one lover...She couldn't find his spirit and he couldn't find her soul...Like adam & eve when they lost it all...Stranger than fiction...Tree blood intervention...Tree of life uprooted...Sacred love deluded...Now the devil looks in her lonely eyes...She kisses back on his lips of lies...What happens when their world breaks like a diamond...Poets go on strike and stop all poems from rhyming...She wants his love, she wants...He wants her love, he hunts...For the shiny stars to always shine...Blood of life their wild moon wine...Can they fall in love, can they fall like the star...They're not trying to become vampires, they already are...Just spinning and wandering in a lost world...

He became the vampire and she the lonely girl...

In Every Blink We Fell In Love Again

The pale lesser light and its beautiful pale tint of love upon usWe cuddled on the beach and gazed at the stars and foot prints on the sand here love was always there Drinking out of Rivers that were lost in the woods with angels and wild wolves, howling in the darkness of light

Our passion and love kissed away that dull and shallow life of forever lightless
It was cold, hot, warm, all in the same sip; where you'll never thirst again;

quivering and shivering eternal love on those romantic lips of glory

Just when we thought we loved hell

We fell in love with Heaven

I kissed you, and I woke up in the Garden of Eden; roses were thorn less and

the world was ours again

You cried one last tear of love… Dripping drops of my faint reflection in the

water of life…I love you was the last tear on my pale face as I stared into your

eyes of eternity and in every blink you were still there, and In every blink

we fell in love again…

My dark heaven
was under your stone light shining
Throbbing dark lust under your pulse ablaze
My harsh dark words in your darker poetry
I felt my stone heartbeat, banging Ezekiel's
bones with stretched dark hands of thieves…
I've seen my dark eyes
in the maiden light reflection of yours
Escaping my dark adultery into your purity
I kissed your rose lips with my dark night tongue

Lilith my love
I found life in your wet dark garden
Beauty in the wild dark howls of wolves…
For now we see through a glass, darkly
I Found all this in a love darker than mine…
All this in a love darker than mine
Darkness hanging on trees of life
Undone blindness in the dark spots of sunlight
Our new world by the door of that one beautiful
dark red tree bleeding
My teeth in the veins of rivers of pouring blood
Strangely called by dark sounds of holy voices
Thinking evolution compromised…Listening for
trumpets of angels
to wake the dust from its dark sleep
Visions of you coming back,
no longer in your dark robe
You were the light of my lonely dark life…
Now not devilish and lonely
For now we see through a glass, darkly
I found all this in a love darker than mine…
All this in a love darker than mine… by the door
of that one beautiful dark red tree bleeding…
"For now we see through a glass, darkly…"

Love Red Mystery…
So I can taste forever…
You make me go Wilde…
Drunk in denial…

Let's go skinny dipping in our ocean of love
Playing hide go seek in the clouds above
I'm hunting you kindly my gothic dearest
In the city where I scream the kingdom's fearless
Now the woods a different story
The dark forest filled with fire & glory
Hypnotized by salted dirty neon lights
I'm persuaded by all those stormy clueless nights
We painted pictures of a thousand sunless moonless years
The devil crying with he's swollen white painful tears
Soak me in your love red mystery
So I can taste forever…

Love red mystery
So I can taste forever
This is the life that almost got better
This is the feel good push lost in a letter
I'll love you over & over my lover
Vine leaves not as good as the blood cover
I can't get you out of my heart and out my head
I'll never forget what you almost said
Let stay in the tattooed forest & kiss a while
All I want to do is make you smile & smile
I feel your darkness that makes the light
I feel your darkness when the day becomes night
I want you…I need you…Let's run away
To a world where angels pray
To a world where no one is embarrassed
To a world where we can finally share this
Your watery lips showering me in honey & ecstasy
The red dripping tree
Blood forever mystery
Soak me in your love red mystery
So I can taste forever
Love red mystery
So I can taste forever…

Before You Open Your Door

I'll fight for you... Before you let me in
I'll show you I l love... Before you let me in
I'll kiss you with life... Before you let me in
I'll put a ring on your heart's invisible finger
Before you open your door
I just want you and nothing more
I love your gothic lavender eyes
You're my little blood gothic butterfly
 let's play in oceans and water slides
Pass the stars where Saturn hides
They said this was all
Broken mirrors and shattered wall
They don't know how to have gorgeous fun
You light me up where there's no moon or sun
They lost the light that made them shine
One day will be ours in a glass of rainbow wine
When angels are signaled to blow the horn
We'll ride the Pegasus and the Unicorn
I love you...I'm so sorry I left you alone
Don't settle for him, your heart's filled with
Gold...To bad there such a thing as story
changer...The vampire bite that took and
changed her... Come see the Yukon Northern
lights...Will you dance with me forever this
night? I want you like the air wants your
breath...Irish warrior who want a good battle
death...Our blood dripping in dreams of red
The tree of darkness where Eve bled

I'll fight for you... Before you let me in...
I'll show you I l love... Before you let me in...
I'll kiss you with life... Before you let me in...
I'll put a ring on your heart's invisible finger...
Before you let me in...
Before you open your door...
I just want you and nothing more...

Undead Me

Do you feel unclean, unwashed,

vanished of your own presence?

Stripped and starved in your own sacred famish

The woman who never feels her feelings

No more moon in your childless veins

Blood magic stirs the faintish cry

Give me my youth again and keep my old soul

My tears have never been kissed by the right lips

Here's my letter

MY LOST VAMPIRE LETTERS

Swimming in the devil's ocean

My blood has become the devil's maple syrup

Now I'm alive

I see vampires everywhere

You held me in that world of death

And I'm not dead, I am not dead

She screamed in ecstasy…

His face turned into complete horror

    Spiritual blood was dripping down her neck

No…Don't die my love

Don't die my love

My Eve…My sweet love of life

She was curled in his arms

In her mind

Evil hung in the tree and lied…

In her heart

Love hung in tree and died…

Her tears ran down like the first waterfall made

Her last tear dropped hit the cursed ground

Roses grew their thorns

She whispered with her last breath

"I've become your Ghost of Eve…

Save our Roses…And …Undead Me…"

Haunted Bleeding Hands

I'll give you roses with thorns,

not to be mean my love.

Just to remind us how

the darkness tries to kill your beauty.

I'll squeeze it, and watch the blood drip down my pale white hand as it covers

our wickedness in a red sacred bath of love.

I'll be the lost vampire, and you the lonely girl, and we'll show the world that

God is alive in the love of who we are and not what we've become…

Red Door Bleeds

In the blood shadow of the wood cross tree

In The Tattooed Forest

where the red door bleeds

Red Chair in the Forest

Come sit in the Red Chair of the Forest

be free…

Sacred Red thirst

Happy or sad the bird whistles throughout time

Dog barking at such strange mysteries and cat chasing rhymes...Ocean splashing pattern waves and tides...Bear awakes from hibernation

 resurrection of life...Rose grows its thorns a romantic... sorrow it brings

Snake cursed ... lost its jewel filled wings

All this beauty ...All this glory sleeping in the dirt

Never to wake again without his sacred red thirst

Knowing time is just a stubborn illusion

Pretty angel that brought all the confusion

Being human just wasn't enough

We traded our souls for dirt & dust

Devil is scared of the ghost knocking at the door

Those who open not so scared any more

All this beauty

All this glory sleeping in the dirt

Never to wake again ...

without her sacred red thirst...

Silky Spell

The sun won't melt our wings tonight.

 The universe has a black hole;

 its magic at its finest.

It sucks you in its wonderful waterfall of lights.

 Heart swollen with honey;

ready to burst it's sweetness of holy ecstasy.

It draws you in

If I were there, my lil gothic butterfly

My sweet Nightingale

 The story would be different, if I was there.

  Thunder and lightning would be our servants and the novelty would last forever with strawberries and cream whipped in passion overflowing into our wine.

 I would drink & be drunk under your wet silky spell. Your eyes like fingerprints telling me We'll fly where magic is at its finest…

Haunted by Vampires & Love

She sees the castle, but I don't

She drinks the river, but I can't

O sister... Have you gone crazy

O sister... I still love you baby

Damn sacrifices to ghostly gods

Like returning vomiting coyote dogs

Have I drunk the veins of many devils

Evil's made up fairy fables

Holiness Hides in Such Dark Places

We Can't See God... Till We Have Faces

Holy haunted Sacred love

Angelwolves howling the night above

You make me dead...You make me good

Hanging in dark bloody wood

Like blood, Like blood, washing us away

Like love, Like love,

now the vampire sees the light of day

We're haunted, we're haunted,

by Vampires & Love

Now I see with eyes unknown

The world has become our crashing Rome

I cannot hear the trumpets blasting sounds

But I can't stop hearing heaven's bloody hounds

Oh Friends of Job you were wrong

You can love jealousy forever

But they can never get along

She screams & squeals heaven's pleasures

Her sweet love that can never be measured

I just want to love her like the Garden of Eden

I just want to stop her lonely heart bleeding

Like brave heart…The man snake slitting her pale throat

Oh sacred light becoming our wild sheep goat

Like blood, Like blood, washing us away

Like love, Like love, now the vampire sees the light of day

We're Haunted… We're Haunted…

By Vampires & Love

Swollen Soul

The mirror doesn't show who you are

The lights are reflecting the fallen star

The pain, the pain, you feel

Reverse psychology fixation appeal

Taste the taste of a swollen soul

But you can't erase the small pain that's dull

Something is wrong…

in my story chapter infidelity Seven

My God…

The life I've lived in chapter twisted Heaven

Will there be at chapter twelve

 and the midnight strike

Can I live again?

In the darkness of Heaven's light

If the birds flew backwards and the bees buzzed me a stinging song

Would the world not see that there's still something wrong?

Where angels are just watching the story unfold

Where demons laugh

 At the story told of God's tears

Thought in the clouds of rain

Where darkness comes

 with no such thing as shame

"Oh twisted heaven",

she cried for twisted heaven without fear

And she called it Love…

But love doesn't answers to selfish ears

Swollen Soul …

EliEl

Across the sea of emerald green,

Farther than my eyes can see……….

Beyond the hope of Your return

past the dark valley of me…..

through the twisted tunnel of branches

and leaves

I hide and stare…..

huddling cold in my naked truth…..

my torn, ravaged soul bare.

There through a diamond mist of tears I see

atop our hill kneeling under

His saving, shady tree….

the shimmering-liquid light

of the Creator of Me….

whispering to the flowers-----each petal bent

to deeply drink HIS breath……changing colors
with each word….

blushing deeply……eternal life assured.

Creatures I named, of His heart and hand….

gentle, furry, speckled and grand....

each gathered to stand....silently stand...

encircling their Master, Maker, and Friend....

wondrously knowing, beyond love's glowing.....

knowing……..forever beyond love's glowing,

His whispered, gentle words….what was coming.

There in His arms, soft pure-white showing....

my EliEl …crystal-bright curious eyes knowing..

tender, innocent, trusting eyes knowing.

Soft Breath of Life words…last song heard…

Creator's kiss….last breath taken….

Love's gentle wind blowing…

Salvation's rich, red blood flowing…….flowing.

Separated from eternity with each drop of blood spent…..splashing on our hill,

dripping down His Saving, shady tree….

my EliEl……….first to die…..for the likes of me.

I wear His pure-white, soft-warm robe…..

ripped from Him and given freely to me.

Written by Wayne Mussatto/Stonelight

Stealing Heaven

I was the man who stole heaven...

Long before your time...

It all started with a cross

and a crowd of angry people...

Screaming tears and blood...

As I hung there in the presence of darkness...

I thought of my past...

Just a little boy with not enough to eat...

Before I even started, I could feel defeat...

With no parents to help my will...

To survive I learned to lie and steal...

Running most of my life...

To find nothing but pain and strife...

I wonder what would it be like to have a friend?

I went to the church to ask for help...

Even as I bowed and knelt...

The Pharisees laughed and kicked me out...

At times they looked for stones to crush me and my sinner bones...

I ran, I ran up the hill…

"I hate everyone" This is how I feel…

Wait…Wait…A Strong soft voice of a man…

Speaking words of choice…

A man talking of love and happiness…

"Blessed are the sad…

Blessed are the humble…

Blessed are those who show mercy…

Blessed are the pure in heart…

Blessed are the children…

People will insult you and hurt you…

They will lie and say all kinds of evil

and you will be happy"

Oh how I wish I could still what this man has!

Late that day I was caught …

I tried to get away…

I stood and fought…

They wrapped me in chains and cut me down

"You're a thief…On a cross you will die"

I am a thief…To this I could not lie

Years went by…I had no more tears to cry

I know my day is coming…I was next

THERE'S NO MORE ROOM…I DON'T WANT TO DIE

But I never really lived

Then again…That strong…Soft voice…

Outside my dark cell…

I saw a man in the hands of hell…

Whipped until his blood spilt…Over and Over…

With no skin on his back…A crown of thorns smashed to his head…

Just when I thought he was dead…

They slashed his face and

spit on his brow and said…

"Here's your king…

Here's your king…

My cell door opened…

It's time to pay for your crime…

They nailed me to a tree…

Next to a man I could hardly see…

The Blood from his eyes...

I wondered why he was crucified...

When I heard him speak...I knew who he was...

"FATHER, FORGIVE THEM...

FOR THEY KNOW NOT WHAT THEY DO."

Why, I cried!!!This man has done nothing...

He speaks of peace...I am the thief...

Jesus, Jesus I want to be who you are...

I want to go where you go...

I'm glad to die with you...

I want to be in your kingdom...

"I TELL YOU TODAY, YOU WILL BE WITH ME IN PARADISE."

I was the man that stole heaven...

The man who stole heaven......

Written by Denny Mussatto

Pretty Forest

The world has a rainbow

She wears it around her neck

To save her from the dead vampire

Love comes to protect

If she would just let me kiss that dirty rust away

Then the water would come all night and all day

Ask Angels to come and play... Our faces turning bright as the demons danced away

In my world there's no such thing as shame

Just the Devil's laugh in the pouring rain

I love her and they call us insane

If Iron turned gold, and water turned white

Then together forever we'll be in the moonlight

Did I mention and did you know

The world that drowned was promised a rainbow

So pretty like the forest that stares at you

So pretty like the forest that's in love with you

...v---v...

Three Dawns of Love

I feel the hounds of heaven's dark shadows
coming for you.
Don't run my lil dark blossom.
Welcome the new night of the
three dawns of love...

Tint of Love
Should I get baptized in you?
Is your ocean a sea of promise?
Does your heart whisper
like the wind of life and fire?
Are you so powerful
that your water doesn't need water
in your moist soft garden?
When you drink a glass of water and it runs
down your dry desert throat; tell me!
Who is the slave to its cold tidal wave of thirst?
v---v did you know that in one sip of water my
love; there's enough molecules
to stretch to the moon?
The pale lesser light

and its beautiful pale tint of love is upon us...

Lisa's Love

If I were to fall in love with one vampire, whose poetry topples me to my knees and paralyzes me with where I stand, it would be this vampire's words rather, than words alone. For I do not even know this prince's true identity nor what robes his life and background, and still, he does not see his princess' own humanity nor doth he know her real name. So then, does love still conquer all when it is blinded by mystery and want? To Lucian by Lisa

Pre-Vampire

My heart is pounding like Pre-Vampire. Striking hard the chords of love, I look at you and my soul bleeds to be one. My Nightingale, My soft skin, lost somewhere in forgotten Eden, where passion made love for the first time. I've gone further than mere mortals. Trifling in brimming lights where souls less monsters only imagine. I can hear your voice like rushing rivers; life's ivory sap of haunted romance and scent. I yearn for you to become what I've become, dancing in love's pale moonlight. Dark Makers' sacred inventions tossed in the ocean of stars and space. I Drank and swallowed the lake of fire, where demons burned my throat by changing the story of life. I long to live and stare at the blaze of the bronze serpent to unearth the everlasting, look my love, look at the bronze serpent and live with me, without those vampire bites and hideous saliva of drunken angels and fading flowers. I found this my love, in a love darker than mine. I found this other darkness that I love, in a love darker than mine. Love with me and let the night be ours forever… Without death slithering in trees…Without death slithering in you and me…

Gothic Butterfly

My heart felt like it was beating a different
world. A different place of darkness that hovered
like shadows of love and a floating Gothic
Butterfly singing her moonlight, in the skies of
mirrors I was enlightened by her voice. Though
so far away, she stared at the moon at night.
He stared at the moon in the day of the blue sky.
Two different worlds, in two different times…
Love is beyond time…Beyond stars…
You see my lil Gothic Butterfly, I feel your wings
brushing me in the gentle breeze, and my heart
felt like it was beating a different world

You'll be my red lips that I fall in love
We crossed the separated waters
and love kept us dry
Killing the giant and keeping us
alive…Multiplying bread
Giving us more than we could fill…Holding the
sun in the sky as time set still
Keeping the brother killer safe the vagabond
Dodging the spear as the harp sings
her sacred song

I won't just let you die my love …I won't just let
you die…I'll be the black bird on the mountain
feeding our love,
You'll be my red lips that I fall in love
Long hair cut and missing eyes…The witch sees
the king in a pagan disguise
Angels become vampires forbidden door
Unlocking mysteries in Gen 6 verse 4
The sorcerer's lucky verse Axe 13 ate
Sacred ghost prophecy can never be late
I won't just let you die my love …I won't just let
you die…I'll be the black bird on the mountain
feeding our love,
You'll be my red lips that I fall in love
When the fire comes we won't be burned away
Swallowed by the whale for another day
The two translated that never sees death's night
He wept bringing His friend back to life
Lying to his father with an arm full of fake hair

Wrestling with angel on top of heaven's stairs

I won't just let you die my love …I won't just let
you die…I'll be the black bird on the mountain
feeding our love,

You'll be my red lips that I fall in love

Day 3

The cold rain falls on me, and I feel nothing. I'm so numb, away from you… You're so quiet right now, my sleeping beauty, my promised red rose. Nov. 13th your Nightingale will sing you a song, and all will be well… Like when the first man saw the first woman, and love was made, and love was passed on to us. We are lights my love; shining like lighting for the world to see. Our love is bright…

When Nothing Made the Blood Factory

Go back in time with me...A place when and where blood was first made...Dark matter, kisses, dust, and magic breathed into the ground, springing forth the red rose of love...Now picture right now, the present... hundreds of scientist, doctors, and nurses working in a laboratories trying to figure at the mystery of blood... All their tubes, vials, chemicals, smoke, all under the microscope...Staring into the bubbling red with purple, and Lavender dyes...Hours upon hours of thoughts and studies...

The way blood can clot the wound, the dam without command...The red river of life flowing through our veins...Red liquid flowing...Pumping your heart, lubricating inside your body...What is this red mystery? Where is this place where blood was first made? Who is the blood maker...The Blood God...

This blood factory in the past that made red juice of life being poured in us like a bottle of wine? Now picture thoughtless evolution taking nothing, and making us all, and everything...I would have loved to have been there when thoughtlessness made this red mystery...I would have loved to have been there when nothing made the red rose of love...

I would have love to have been there when nothing made the blood factory...

Wild Moon Blood

I'll drink you with my eyes

Staring at the red stone in the sky

For many,

the taste of the death will be dusty and good...

For me I'll taste your faith that's just misunderstood

I drank the wild moon blood

Drunk with trickery white shadowy lies

You could hear the city scream her dragon cry

She tried walking away,

looking back, turning into salt...

Dragged out by angels, my vampire waltzes

I begged for your kiss...My lips missed your lips

I'm still here drinking Wild Moon reminisce

Oh how I love the taste,

but it never quenches my thirst

Not like you did...Not like you hurt

Where are those horses in the clouds, to come and drink this Wild Moon Blood away?

Buzzed by the red stone lullaby

The tide in my heart is a wicked ocean

coming alive

I drank you... Now I'm swallowed by you

Wild Moon Blood and the Demons Quiver

Drinking my Death was the Lion in the River

Kael Quotes

"In the darkness the trees are full of starlight and I know it's only in my mind. I am talking to myself, not to him. I love him, but the night is over, he's gone."

"You're right...We are beings of light...We're children of the moonlight sucking the light out of the sun..."
Kael, at the Library with Lucian

The Wolf Eye...

I like the wolf's eye better than the alligator's eye. The Wolf's eye is wild with beautiful howling poetry behind it, mysteriously showing Love's wild side. That Narnia girl wasn't sure if she could drink the water with the lion in the river. The Lion told her, there was nowhere else to go. A sure sacred frightening saving disaster and truth that will swallow the world...

Christian Vampire

A Christian Vampire is the one that wants the blood but not the person... You want Grace so that you can push the nails in harder...

Ontologically Haunting

I want to express this ontologically haunted feeling that I have with the universe... I'm such a hopeless romantic mystic... Running trying to catch the Three Dawns...

Eve's Lonely Forgotten Tear

The wicked witch laughed at my pain....

Her spell became my dark fame

You see, I see, pass I see...

Into the vein rivers that washed into the sea

If only my blood would have

turned like frog's skin

This love... My love... Is a different kind of sin

Killing me with your darkness

The dragon screams you're heartless

2 kinds of losses...2 kinds of crosses

Every morning the moon seems to go away

Every night I look up and

wonder who made the made

I cried for burning witches, just to please them and thee

We became God killers...

When we nailed him to the red door tree

If I just kept kissing you the witch would have never burned

If I just kept kissing you,

this tragic life would be unlearned

I didn't know that day I said good bye

That it would curse the world

and we all would die

For everything I've done,

you still tell me not to fear

But I can't help drinking…

Her Forgotten Tears…

The Stone Cracked Table

I'm willing to drown in the sun light, even if it burns me away. The dark glass haunting,will make me again someday.

There's only one answer to all of life's problems,

The trump card that will shock all of evil!

It was done when the stone tabled cracked.

Heaven's Dark Shadow

Come with me before midnight strikes,

it's only eleven

I want to personally invite you

To Lucian's dark heaven

Quiet Tippy Toes

You cry, you cry, and so do I...
Same blood tears...
Different colored eye...
You try, you try, and so do I...
Broken wings unfixed can never fly...
Is the earth Young or is it Old?
Trapped together in a timeless Soul...
Why can't she just let him go...Don't ask her,
she doesn't know...
In the darkness, quiet tippy toes...
LOVE ALWAYS...
Mr. Who!!!Nobody knows...
You see, you see, and so do I...
Broken fallen mirrors we try to hide...
I want, I want, and so do you...
To fall, just fall...In the lake of blue...
Your heart, my heart, the beats are true...
Not on time like we wish them too...
Why can't he just let her go...?
Don't ask him... He doesn't know...
In the darkness, quiet tippy toes...
LOVE ALWAYS...
Mrs. Who!!! Nobody knows...
Can someone please break the spell...
Dirt and dust playing hard to tell...
Look lock blues and brown...
Only they know why the stare down
They love us, they love us not...
Jealousy, kill the flowers is the story plot...
Why can't they just let them go...Don't ask
them...They'll never know...
In the darkness, quiet tippy toes... LOVE
ALWAYS... Mr. & Mrs. Who!!!
Nobody knows...

Lucian quotes Rich Mullins...

"Tonight, not only do I find this world frightening - I am frightened of myself. I am frightened of the evil that I am capable of. I am frightened of that which You (I believe) would deliver me from, and yet I will won't let go. Help me to let go... "Deliver us from evil...From moral duplicity and weakness, from laziness and spiritual complacency, from those lies we tell ourselves from our fear of facing the truth. I think my love that we're all afraid of werewolves - not afraid of being destroyed by one – afraid of being one."

Signs of Immortality... Written by a searching soul

1st sign of immortality– have you ever notice that a man and woman can come together and create a new person, together you create new baby flesh, but strangely enough you cannot keep your own skin new or from growing old? You can create a new flesh, but you cannot keep you own flesh from growing old. So in front of you own eyes; life goes on with another soul that has new skin... It's like immortality goes on without you, right in front of you, even though it was in you that created something new. So close to the secret of life, but somehow separated...

Could it be a curse?

2nd sign of immortality– The spark of life has to be greater than death itself. Think about it, the very fact that we are alive is a sign of immortality. Life is always greater than death because death is nothingness. Death did not make life; life was before death, so life is greater... Since life made life, and life was first, and then death was second. (Could there be a curse?). How can death create anything? It can't, death is nonexistence. So for us to be here; there must have always been life. Something must have always been; for us to be. Life...The spark has always been and the spark will always be; since it was never created. "

The law of conservation of energy.

States that energy can be neither created nor destroyed."

3rd sign of immortality– After the winter of death, there is the life of spring, now I feel this is more of a sign of resuscitation or recovery, but nevertheless it is also a sign that life can be saved. Some may see this as reincarnation, but I see this as a sign of resurrection… The flowers that seems dead in the winter, still has its roots; and spring comes and feeds life again. Something that can make something live again (Anthropic Principle) is a sign of immortality. Why does the flower die? And why do beautiful roses have thorns? I heard it said that roses have thorns because over millions of years of picking and in the evolution process roses decided grow thorns; so they wouldn't get picked. So I'm thinking, if roses can think to grow thorns, I was wondering if it ever thought about growing tiny little machine guns to protect themselves (bang, bang). Roses having thorns, does that sound like evolution or does that sound like a curse?

4th sign of immorality– I believe is written in the hearts of us all. The old sacred book says in Ecclesiastes 3:11 "eternity in the hearts of men".

In Don Richardson book Eternity in their hearts, he studied cultures throughout the world and found within hundreds of them startling evidence of the belief in eternity in their hearts and in one true God. If eternity is in our heart, then we have a desire to live forever. C.S. Lewis said "Atheism turns out to be too simple. If the whole universe has no meaning, we should never have found out that it has no meaning.

5th sign of immortality– Is the Stonelight…

They saw him in public execution in front of a huge crowd and He was crucified between two thieves, and as the sun was going down they came to break his legs and the thieves to make sure they we're dead; That's when they saw that he had already died; but to make sure they thrust a spear into His side and water came gushing out of His side…
The blood and the water separated;
 Jesus was dead!
They wrapped him up like a mummy and placed in a tomb and rolled a thousand pound stone to cover is grave…

The roman soldier remembering and hearing; that He would come back from the dead in three days. So they told Pilate. Pilate was the one that had him executed and Pilate told the guards to guard the tomb and if anyone stole the body they were to be executed and the roman soldiers would be executed with them…

Some of those who loved him came to anoint His body; on the third day; but when they got there the stone was rolled away and he was gone and there lying neatly was the wrapping. It looked as if He had just disappeared…

The roman soldiers said they fainted in the presence of a super natural being. They saw the stonelight, but the guards were paid off to keep quiet about it and on their behalf the ones who wanted Him dead would tell the people a different story to save the soldiers' lives…

Loved ones wanted to tell everyone about the Stonelight; His Resurrection from the dead the greatest thing they ever saw, and most of them where killed for it. This is strange because before he was dead, His loved ones wouldn't have died for Him even though they saw Him perform many miracles or you might call it

  true magic…

It wasn't until they saw Him alive again, that they were willing to die for Him. They we're so dramatically changed from being so cowardly before; to being brave ones and willing to die for what they saw.

They saw The Stonelight.
They saw Jesus back from the dead.
It wasn't just the roman soldiers and His loved ones that saw Him alive again; it was reported that 500 other people had seen Him too.
But was He just a ghost?

No... The old sacred book says He ate with His friends and one follower even put his fingers in the wholes of Jesus' hands, and in His side; where the spear had pierced Him. The rest who didn't believe well they have never did find the body of Jesus,
but for those who research the story,
and they found it to be true...

Phantoms of God

It's raining blood…

Drips into puddles and splashes

Like the devil's flood…

Drips from the back lashes

The blood flower buds…

Planting the immortal seed

I walk through the tattooed forest and

 followed you

Through the red door……

I disappeared into the woods of heaven

I left the city of New York crying…

 Her earth veins were like rivers…

Shattered…

From the fallen cut hairs of angels...

Once upon a time….

The Blood Maker comes

Breathe into the dust once again…

Into us… In us… Re-Make us…

Phantoms of God…

Dark Woods of House 123

The mysterious blue vampire light

In the window of dark wonder

Walking down W. 1st Street

Passing by where haunted and beauty meet

Where can you go?

Frightened and Blessed

Sitting on the stairs of deathly hollow

Dante, Dante, I'm here in your dark woods

Walk with me if you can,

 if you would, if you should

See the frameless window of the August sky

There's your magic, there's your sublime

Come see the rock made by the giant

The Sun is peaking under the nightfall

Walk with me back down the hill

Under the night…

Wine, passion,

heat, lovers, with no certainty…

Surprise me…

Only The watchers… Watching…

Outside the house of 123…

Are you haunted? Are you loved?

Surprise me…

Dark Woods of House 123

Dark Kiss
Oh… Your dark lips…
I just want one gothic kiss…
Your powdered face painful story…
Black has become our backwards glory…
My red lips like a bleeding rose…
Your High black boots with pointed toes…
Nails are dark like the black queen of spades…
I love romance, not the fifty grays of shades…
You better than all that…
Your better than all this…
And all I want…
Is just one gothic kiss…
How lucky can I be…
To feel the suffocating of thee…
I'm dying…You're dying…We're dying…
Black tongue with a vampire hiss…
All I want lover is just one dark kiss…
From your pale face…Black lips
Don't let me die and miss…
Oh...Just One…
Dark Kiss…

Angel Poet I

Don't Touch This Heart, It's Already Gone. If You Want This Kiss, Wait Till The Darkness Of Dawn. The Deeper You Go, The More You Will Want. But Every Night Your Dreams My Nightmares Will Haunt. You Can Feel My Touch, You Can Take In My Soul. I Live In That Broken Tree With The Darkest Small Hole…- My Angel Poet…

Angel Poet II

Would You Let Me Die
 If That Was The Only Way?
Take My Hand,
Touch My Hair, The Way You Play
Will We Pass Those Trees, Those Dark Shadows Of The Night?
Will You Cover My Eyes To Save Them From That Hateful Sight?

Imagery

The natural darkness praises the moonlight through the wild eyed wolf, who is howling to the blood maker is like Biblical Imagery

Dark Mirrors

I live in a very colorful dark world
In a world full of stones,
 coffins, moonlights, and trees
The grass isn't green on the other side...
It's see through...I've seen the white shadows
Angelwolves in the eyes of my heart
They cross through my untrusting paths
Drinking the different shades of Sacred wine...
Spills in my Golgotha heart
I Drank...What the devil's made...
Dark mirror...You've seen them...Haven't you?
Staring as you comb your hair
Haunted by the clowns under your skin
You've felt the touch of your pale child ghost
Lingering fading memories...You've seen their faces worn backwards
Haven't you taste the strawberries of God?
Untainted blood... Scared and begotten
The dead seeking for your death
The hell in you screams at the demons of heaven
Killed before you were born...
Splashing water on your lifeless face
Zombie Face...
    I live in a very colorful dark world
    In a world full of stones,
    coffins, moonlights, and trees
    I live in a world of Dark mirrors
    You've seen them haven't you

    Dark Mirrors...

Vampire Rush

People always want the mighty rush of becoming a vampire. What about the rush being a pure human without the darkness?

Lucian's Song of Songs II

Sexy Lil Quivers

Red curtains with moonlight blood…

Dark sheets with moonlight love…

The snow is coming… Such a white little thrill…Hot chocolate lovers… Amatory chill…Can't kill death… Though we'll try…The early vamp mist… Angels do die…Lucian loves me… Marry me Wilde…

Haunting me with your red prolific style…All these thoughts and all this thinking…Not enough drinks… So I can't stop drinking…

Oh my Star lights are calling your name…Roasting marshmallows by your passionate flame…A little scotch and a little eggnog….

A little of you and a little play god…

Here comes the fall…Here comes the rivers…

Just shaking there with those Sexy Lil Quivers…

Sexy Lil Quivers…

Bitten by Lucian Wilde…v---v…

Hollow Man

Snowy white beautiful red
Where vampire butterflies bled

Frost bitten by snow white

She fills my heart with cold delight

The white straps with a red bow

She makes the fire burn and glow

She brings the wolf out inside of me

She makes me wish I was the frost on the tree

Where can a find such a beautiful woman

That I can love…like no other woman

Should I re-write the songs of King Solomon?

So your love can fill up this hollow man

Redless

My lost dark dove...Careful my gothic dark love
Who I'm I? Don't blink an eye
You're still like a child
Become a Wolf with the Wild
Black forest with silver light
Come my love... So very quiet
Don't let them see us...Our red bleeding sea dust
Checkmate...I got you now
Beautiful eyes...Mirror me round
I drank you like the river falls
I love you like the death of us all
I kissed you and lived a thousand stolen stories
I want you...Like God wants holy glory
Oh my...I can't take this
Run my love...I see Redless...
I've become so heart less
Like the cross...love hanging groundless
Your broken wings... Were Angel clipped
Your heart fell down... Your spirit slipped
Now you're no longer a child
Bitten by Lucian Wilde...
Why did you look so delightful
Why were your lips so tasteful

Oh my…I can't take this
Run my love…Before you're bloodless
Okay, okay… I Promise… Just one Kiss
Oh my love…I see …Redless…

Quieter Tippy Toes
Cry, I, Colored Eye
Try, I, Fly
Young, Old, Soul
Why, Go, She Doesn't Know
In the Darkness Quieter Tippy Toes
You See, I, Try to Hide
I want you, Fall, In the Lake of Blue
Your Heart, My Heart, Wish them too
Why, Go, He Doesn't Know
In the darkness, quiet tippy toes
Break Spell, Dirt Dust, hard to tell
What's this mystery…What's this spell?
They love us, they love us not
Jealousy kills the flowers… The story plot
Let them Go…They'll Never Know
In the darkness, quite tippy toes…

Bloody Soap Bubbles
Breathe me in… But never breathe me out
Haunted by Eden without the glow
Wrapped in ivy clover so our skin won't show
Let's take it all off and bathe in waters of red
Bloody soap bubbles that wake the forever dead
A love unto life and a love unto death
Which love will you love
 when you take your last breath?
I'll be your poet of fame,
your bronze serpent of glamour
Look at me,
 my love won't be the one that damns her
I'll go in and out of the dark
In and out of her shadowy heart
Making you feel
On the grassy hill
My world at ease
Your world a tease
You don't see me, I don't see you
Not us… but the other two
You never gave me a real chance
You thought I needed just a one night dance
You're drinking streams and I'm drinking rivers
In the cold where the white demon shivers

Moonless Parable

"The sky was twisted purplish and grey gone wrong...It seemed like the whole world was singing the wrong song...Kites were entangled in the fractured sunless sky...Mirrors were showering broken faces of goodbyes...They prayed to the moon, prayers bouncing off shameful clouds...No one could hear each other, it was screaming violently loud...The confusion was us feeling the fake drunken clown...

The cats came out to have their eyes for dinner...Demons stopped laughing when the darkness began to quiver

Rivers started streaming backwards...
The gravity push felt downwards...
I love you only came from the mouth of a doll...
I hate you came out of the mouth of us all...The ones that thought they were soulless, where about to be soulless...Like a wolf howling thinking they were moonless; now moonless...
Don't tell me you think you know what hell is...
You took everything away from what was his...
Now she has nothing and no time to forgive...
Making up reincarnation for another chance to live...The red soup bowl hot and ready to go...

Dark Angels praying for God to let it snow…Wake up reader you're living in Lazarus's parable…You can't wake up now… Inescapable…She so beautiful…

She so irresistible…I went out and thought of the unthinkable…I grabbed her hand and kissed her good bye…She told us we believed in The lie…She kissed my lips and wouldn't let me leave…We all confessed and fell to our knees…He so handsome that flawless angel of light…She's the one who loved me, and she's the one who's right…I wanted to kiss the groom's beautiful wonderful bride…All of them were on there on that side…She's already left Lazarus…She's already gone over the wall…You mean this was a moonless parable after all?"

The darkness scattered in the night…
The poetry left the lesser light…
The rhyme was no more...
The ground had no floor...
How do you get out of a moonless parable?

Black Dungeon as a Heart

If we could only be reborn again
 with pure blood from the start...
Then we wouldn't have to wear
 a black dungeon as a heart...
Like the wicked men that sold her
Your cheap dark smoke disowned her
Slow death by the moon
The midnight trial you called witchery afternoon
Innocent trial covered in darkness
You tried to hide loves most highest
You killed life, and then you begged for it
Thorns and slashes, you cast lots for it
You're dumb and blind... Wake up dead man
You thought science was the only genesis plan
Studying the gold
 that was already here to tempt the eye
Studying silver that killed the werewolf inside
Watching hairs turn white and gray
You never found the truth,
and you think that's okay
Vampires killed truth
 and love and hung it in trees
You thought it was you that killed the
magnificent thee
It's not against flesh and blood that you wrestle
Born in your right religion of how I'm so special
I'm not sure...I know everyone's blood is cursed

There's a few who have a sacred blood thirst
I'm looking where Eve's blood was first spilled…
Where vampires took another Adam;
 with a cross He was killed…He was right…
Love salt full of light…
We must to be born again
With blood that hasn't been contaminated
with vampire sin
If we could only be reborn
 with pure blood from the start
Then we wouldn't have to wear
 a black dungeon as a heart

Almost Jealous

I was almost jealous
when the clock struck twelve
Almost jealous when you kissed the little elve
I was almost jealous of that sexy picture
Almost jealous of the half man next to her
I was almost jealous
of the gate that was open to him
Almost jealous when the lights went dim
Dreaming of me in my words of my moonlight
Dreaming of me when the day
turns gothic midnight
Thunder flashes and rain falls
against your pale skin
For that little moment
 when you're not thinking of him
When dreaming is over and it's just not enough
Smoking those cigarettes
 with your smoker's cough
Every buzz you try doesn't buzz like me
You want my shadow
to come and set your heart free
Now back to making your down-town lips water
Trying hard not to kiss king's beautiful daughter
Those mortal men
want to put a stake in my heart
I'm your little hidden secret in your quiet dark
You know I will always be your lighted candle
Knocking and shaking your dreamy handle

I was almost jealous
of the gate that was open to him
Almost jealous when the lights went softly dim
Almost jealous…
But I know how you want to be free
I was almost jealous
but I know you really love me

...Unvampilized...

The nightingale screams as you watch it bleed

With hands pressed against the red door tree

Come bring your wishes and curses

Your spirit aches and your heart breaks

Your kingdom come your will undone

Your skate board and your scars

Your nasty finger and screaming guitars

Feeling so sorry for yourself trashy story

Human rights with all its dirty glory

Your blood shadow of the wood cross tree

Your Tattooed Forest where the red door bleeds

The happiness you claim but you never had

Fabulous Unholy nights... All turned bad

The nightingale screams as you watch it bleed

With hands pressed against the red door tree

Is there such a thing as a new creature?

The Nightingale again flies...

Empty grave yards...

The demons spoils are Unvampilized...

… It Never Snows on the Sun …

Riding my car off the midnight waterfall

Drowning in the devil's love letter

I thought I was getting better

You say it's all just fine

Perfect… Let me poor you another glass of wine

I'm I saying this to you?

Are you saying this to me?

You don't know who you are?

I'm the serpent hanging in the tree

Good one Lucian the rebel…

Good one Satan you Devil

You're so courageous and you're so brave

To believe the devil's souls can still be saved

I tasted dragon lips of gold, when the clock struck eleven

There's no such place as Soulless Heaven

You can hide and you can run

But it never snows on the Sun

Day 4

Remember our midnight swims in the middle of Coeur D'Alene Lake, and running around Tub's Hill... You were like thief that was promised paradise, steeling my soul with every touch, and every look. You almost crashed the plane that night, but I could have died right then and there with you; destiny has its wild strange ways. Our flight through New York City; I hear your laughter and your screams of joy... Tears drops of magic potion the leaks the goodness of life. Signs of a tear maker, so it seems, making tears of love that's not forgotten in the wind of fate. If there was such a person capturing all the tears that I've missed?
I would give my soul for every drop!

Green Monarchs
The Green Monarchs keep me invisible...
The blood experiment makes me more alive...
It's beautiful up here;
looking down on my moonlit ocean...
I've been bitten by wolves,
their dead green eyes...
I'm bitten by the loss of you,
and I cry tears like God's tears
to flood my world away...
I miss you Kael...

**Very Quiet Tippy Toes
LOVE ALWAYS... Mr. & Mrs. Who...
Nobody Knows...
They love us, they love us not...
Jealousy kills the flowers... The story plot...
Let them Go...They'll Never Know...
In the darkness, <u>Shhh Tippy Toes</u>**

: ... "..." ... :
Blood Magic Stir

We're becoming more than human
More than what we were
Your blood... My blood... Blood magic stir
Your howling wolf... Maiden eye stares
How beautiful our blood forever to share
Dreaming of Sandpoint Mountains
And New York City lights
Forever lightless transcendent crystal nights
Passion, the beginning of sublime
You and I to complete the Neo-rhyme
One who eats became something to eat
Out of the strong came something sweet
The riddle of a short haired eyeless man
The honey lion fox killer burned the land
We're becoming more than human...
More than what we were
Your blood... My blood... Blood magic stir
I need you, I love you like food
Once upon a time, timeless good
Our static is better than the northern lights

Manhattan vampire pre-flights
Here's the sudden steal
Here's the Blood thirsty kill
Oh yeah we died to ourselves
Oh yeah we're dead…
Like the dead curse tree door that slowly bled
The day became midnight, the sky sacred tears crying
The rose grew thorns, life slowly dying
Three days later all tears one day will be done…
The moon has become our darker blood God son…
We're becoming more than human…
More than what we were
Your blood… My Blood…Blood Magic Stir…

Vampire Thirst

Your mystical blood so wonderfully red
Blood so full of love like you said
When I taste you…I tasted heaven alacrity
Poured in my soul sick animosity
Magical water falls from the sky
The dry earth begins to wipe her eyes
Red roses grow from the ground
Twisted thorns & bleeding crown
The end is coming…The time is near
How did Enoch just disappear?
Short of the love where the devil dangles
Dragons and feathers of stolen angels
Mystical Blood…Bring life to her soul
Vampire thirst… Eve's deathly fall
Mystical Blood…Blood God soul
Vampire thirst… Is killing us all
You don't believe… The whole world is crying
You don't believe…Then why are you dying?
Vampire Thirst…Has left her needing
Vampire thirst… Has kept you bleeding

Religion

**Religion is a haunted Ghost Story
…That haunts the souls of its believers…**

Burnless Vampire

Blood Eyes…In the Colors of Madness

Holy vase catching your gray tears of sadness

Lake of fire was blazing in your eyes

Twilight cracked your screaming throat's cry

White shadows dying moonless night

No spirit to hold your drunken daylight

Your blue heart couldn't take the red any longer

Infected blood

pushing to get the white demon stronger

Midnight days of being born for the first time

Confusion proposing the thorny godless wine

You couldn't see dust & dirt

were playing hard to tell

Watching those black days

chase those white days to hell

You only wanted love!

Insanity became your push and your shove

Rivers of serpent...

Your flow less veins frozen

What happens when your destiny isn't chosen?

You say you were so lightless, no lighting struck

Where was love

when I gave my soul to pure luck?

"What's the Secret Lucian" ask the vampires

What do we do?

How does a vampire not burn

the sun is coming soon

You want to know what I did...What I do?

The sunlight became my yellow lake moon...

How do I do, what you did, what you do?

I gave my unsacred darkness

to blood maker's moon!

Baptized in imagination

with the stonelight above

Now I dance in the darkness we call sacred love

Hurry, hurry... Here comes my dark hour

Don't worry my love; I'm a Burnless Vampire

Blacker Veil

Here comes the death kiss...

Here comes the love...

Here comes that sweet angel...

Cooking in your stove...

lick lips & dip...

In her She-wolf cell...

Hot tongue pushing

In her wishing well...

Freeing the butterfly from the jar...

I love you... And your deep chiseled scar...

Your dark prince of light...

Goodbye sun Goodnight...

Vampire knows

The Vampires know

No sun...no SUN

Not a fairytale...

Just our love...Dark story...

Lucian's Song of Songs III
    (Drip Drop Bliss)

I can't stop kiss kiss kissing

Your watery lips

I keep stick sticking

Drip drop drips…

Not one inch of you to waste

Your sweet honey taste

Oh dreamy place

Drip drop kiss…

Can't stop now

Can't stop how

Drown me in your dripping pond

Sing me another song

Your luscious lips

Your curvy hips

Such a tasty sip

Such a beautiful slip

Give me…Give me

Drip Drop Bliss…

The Blood Maker

Eyes glared haunted estranged
Light dimmed smile deranged
Soul trade soulless price
Somewhere stolen midnight twice
Wolf cries moon has died
Tears swollen lips have lied
White snow turning black…
Grace love given back
Blood drips tonight with splashes
Demon scratching Angel's rashes
Snakes breathing dirty dust
Lost wings Earth's crust
The Vampires come to take her
Help us find the blood maker
Flowers fading in the dark
Stake pierced in her bleeding heart
Naked skin pale and white
Dark traded yellow light
She's surrounded still alone
Emptiness ache's lifeless bone
Love Forgive us whoever you are
knife…Bleeding out my only life
Eve drops her red rose thorn
Cross hands nailed and torn
The Vampires come to take her
Help us find the blood maker

Whispering Trees

Our vampire wave…Peace finger by the neck

Poets are not of anything…Like the joker in the card deck…You told me to remember their scolding rules…Like swords men gathering at a gentlemen's duel…You were the last person I hugged that night…Like fire blazing in the silver moonlight…Others jealous of us…

We're not of time

Love untouched…Such a romantic Devine

You say timeless treasures must remain buried

Lost his soul when he forgot he was married

You don't want to affect me…I've become such a fool….Just watch for the wolves Lucian… Such beautiful wool

Thinking I'm a sheep in wolves clothing

Please just don't lose yourself in the rubble of nothing…Remember the blood God and don't get lost Like desperation… Trying not to get caught…Now you're crying and counting the stars…Oh my…

I'm just trying to name the voices thus far

What I'm I then? Do you want the howling to stop?

Oh no…Have you already forgot

Whispering Trees… Sing us your chorus

Whispering Trees… Tell us about your forest

Whispering Trees love blowing in the leaves

Whispering Trees… Oh whispering trees

Day 5

The world whispering that there's more to life, but I'm still so lonely here without you. Is there no other voice to tell me that we'll be okay? Every one lies. Those who say there is a God; lie! Those who say there is no God; lie! We're all liars, but I didn't want to be one of them, and I still won't my love; my silence, my promise fulfilled as you bud into what I promised; it's all I think when I disappear into you.

Zombie Blood

Your Zombie blood down my lips…
Your life in veiny sips…
Dark forest… Thousands of roots…
Come wear the devil's white angel boots…
Dragon owl… Howls a whooshing sound…
The gospel of love buried in the dirty ground…
Alive, but count yourself as dead…
Zombie death has bled & bled…
No more spirit, no more soul…
The devil's teeth are filled with your gold…
Who are you? The drinking dead
 Just a passing flower's unfaithful friend…

Atheist Kiss…

My mind would say there is no God,

but my soul is haunted by a different story…

This earthy life we live is…

Touched by a cold stream…

Felt in a little girl's smile…

Tickled by a black man's laugh…

Tasted in toast and butter…

October's Blue moon…

Wings of angels…

Our wishful imagination…

Puzzles and Kisses of Heaven…

Even in our darkest of pain…

Bleeding hands, thorns, romance, lust less shadows…

A cross that says, all of this…

All of this is where love and evil have found salvation…

Life and death pressing its lips together…

Here we feel the kiss, and now my mind agrees with my haunted soul

that we feel the kiss…

Try to live this earthy mysterious life with aching souls

for the kiss that will awake us all…

For now we kiss like atheist…

But soon we'll kiss like God…

After Twilight
I swear by my skin
That our souls are rotting away
The flame of hell has dried up all our Seas
If I could take all our tears we ever cried
Reborn the ocean and make us alive
I swear by my bones
We're not alone
We dress ourselves like the evil of the night
Oh invisible, can you see our faces
With just a candle light
I swear by my spirit
That I could hear it
The ghost of a sacred lingering
Haunted by demons
By their heavy breathing

After
After
After Twilight

Oh invisible faces, can you see our faces
With just a candle light in these dark places

After After Twilight…

The World Past Heaven

My one Dark Wish
Is in the world past heaven
My eyes are closed, hands open
I cast my wish into the dark wishing well
And dove in after it
I sank into dusty breaths of holy lovers
Sensations of phantom fingers are better than winds
Voices of trees I hear in every branch
Corinthians' leaves telling us the story of 2:9
The wolves' teeth are like treasures
Howling wild moonlight... The dark face of God
Once upon a timeless...She loved him perfectly
Once upon a timeless...He loved her in every way
Oh... Hear the sun say something yellow
Misty gold...Green soothing blues of enchantment
White beautiful shadows before they became darkly
Thirsty flowers drinking the mornings' unspoiled dew... Every petal kissing kisses of unfallen love
Isaiah's verdures branches and leaves telling the story...Many mansions house address sixty six and twenty two...My one dark wish...
In the world past heaven...
My one dark wish...Is to hear you say...
"I sank into dusty breaths of sacred lovers...
Sensations of phantom fingers are better than winds..."

Moon Burn

If you get a moon burn it will make your skin a light white palish grey and your heart a faintish tint of blue…Perfectly naked with the winds of everything… So calm, calming the gentle flowing streams. Our perfect kisses in the midnight with stars of jealousy's bliss… Hedonist lovers rolling in the grassy hills…We fall into a deep trance and breathe the night away… Here comes the sun poking out its yellow eye, and the darkness begs for forgiveness and flees into the white shadows…Into drops of love and drops of gold mist…The earth sweats the morning dew of last night's luscious lips of holy lust…Fresh, clear and clean, into drops of love, into drops of gold mist, without the burnt smoke of devils…But soon the moon will appear again and the yellow light will sleep with one eye open that reflects upon the mysterious stone rolled away into the sky…Our resurrection has come again, just like the night before…I will kiss you all over again…And I will love you all over again…and I will pray that the sun will sleep just a little longer tonight, so we can lay down by the rivers and drink from the little brooks of wine as we exchange our potions…Come my love…Come get a Moon Burn in our naked endless love…The story will never end as long as the author writes new chapters…Chapter 1, 777 moon burn forever…Only for a little while will I have to let you go, but soon you will be my moon flower forever…Chapter 7, 777 Moon Flower Resurrection…

Our resurrection has come again,

but this time its forever…

Chapter endless has come my love…

Haunted by the Basement Door
Woke up early from a reckless night
Wasn't ready to see the sunlight
Poured my coffee and lit up my cig
Could remember last night what I did
There's this silence in the Bad Lands
I blew out all the candlelight lampstands
To be no more… To be no more
I opened up the haunted basement door
I washed the rings around my dark eyes
In the mirror I saw ONLY terrible lies
Cold with icy blood
Goodbye My Love
Meet the devil no more
I can feel my body lifting off the lifeless floor
I'm here, where no one can tell
Casting my dark wish in the dark wishing well
STONELIGHT…
Shinning out of the DARK haunted basement floor
Shining forever… Forever more
Haunted Basement Door

Dark Tree

I remember when you loved me
I remember it all
I remember it like heaven
I remember the fall
Now I sit here in disbelief
Just remembering how you loved me
Can I make it up to you?
Besides hanging on a dark tree
Can I believe like I did
Back when I was free
I still want your love, I really do
I still want... All of you
You've saved me a thousand times,
 maybe just once more
I should have known
That was you knocking on the door
I was told to never answer doors in dreams
Nightmares foretold and devil screams
Oh Thee... Oh Thee...Hanging on a dark tree...
Oh me...Oh me...Hanging on a dark tree...
Now I've become afraid of it all...I know why I'm here
The man hanging next to me is crying god's tears

Darkest of Ink
Flowing from the poet's brush
Writing me away
You know I've always loved you
I just had to see
If you were there in my blood
You pushed the Stone away
Till the night became the day
The Love I've always wanted
The love
The Darkest of Ink
Writing me away

Dark Poets Die Young
Woe unto you... Woe
Thou art the dark Edgar Allan Poe
Sweet symphony & musical art
32 & dead the incredible Mozart
Here comes the darkness crashing in our minds
Making us insane... The devil's dark wine
Here comes death...The screaming choker
Now he's dead, Heath Ledger the joker
Mr. Wilde introducing the Dark poet Oscar
Alcohol spins your mind like a crashing helicopter
Death has stung...Death has stung
All Dark Poets die young
In haunted minds darkly blazing
Doc Holiday...Huckleberry and I'll be your daisy
Billy the kid and Nietzsche, they all went crazy
God is dead... No! "We Are" said the three of I
And I'll be the next dark poet to die
But before I die... I was chosen
I'm still alive...yours truly, Beethoven

Holy Loneliness

What if we're all wrong
What if we don't lust and lie for reasons we believe
What if we sold our souls, but never wanted to
I only say what if... I can't speak for others
Why do we make scars on love
Why do we make scars on each other?
What if our true desire is to be pure, but we can't
And because we can't we feed the evil hunger of desire
If you could be anything you wanted
What are your true colors
A vampire or pure human?
Wait a minute; this is a real fight
We have always been bent in both directions
how is it that being a vampire
is more of a thrilling thought?
Being pure human sounds even more impossible
Not often thought of
Where I'm I going with all this
Could it be that all our evilness and darkness is truly just a cry of being lonely?
Could that loneliness be a cry for something greater and more beautiful that what we've become...
"BUT Wait A Minute" "I Want To Be Evil..."
Okay, but that's what WE can been...
Being a pure human, we have never known
So could our cry really be a cry of... Holy Loneliness?

Jesus Skeleton

I can taste the blood in my mouth
But the skeletons I cannot find
Oscar Wilde said, "You are everywhere."
Did the dogs come and drag your body away?
Mankind is still searching and cannot find your bones
I can taste the blood in my mouth
But the skeletons I cannot find
What scares me is the ladies left bleeding in the trees
And the dragon owl is chasing the red dove
History calls you a magician…Has your bones disappeared in the dust?
Has Elymas come to delude the world?
What we hate is words…Words that are made alive
What set us free…Words that are made alive
The vampire changes shape in the darkness of night
Bending its invisible dusty bones
Appearing only to find a stake in its heart
White demon love song has drank the Twilight away
Napoleon said, "I know men, and I tell you that Jesus Christ is not a man."
Those angelwolves howl away all night long

Those phantoms of god are jealous of your flesh

And I can taste blood, but I cannot find your bones

The pure genius said, "You can shut Him up for a fool, you can spit at Him and kill Him as a demon; or you can fall at His feet and call Him Lord and God."

I love the woods of heaven

Where I can play hide go seek with the glory of love

I hide behind heaven's trees

Looking and looking to see if I can look at you

I can't see your skeleton

But I do see blood dripping from your hands………Jesus Skelton

Black Heaven

When I saw her, she rocked my world
Where can I find such a beautiful black pearl
I thought this place was only gold and light
I never thought of heaven as being the night
Saturday school blinding lights
Sunday school more blinding lights
This is Dark with lovely nights
Shadows of heaven such a beautiful sight
My heart of darkness turned shadowy white

Hidden in the nights of love, just me and her
Oh black heaven is more than I deserve

I saw the place where love made wild
I watched god make moons with different styles
Wolves came up from the golden ground
Howling at the blood god with angel sounds
My heart filled up like a romantic flood
My heart sang with the little black dove
Where else can you find such a beautiful dark place
Here in the hills of red sacred grace

Hidden in the nights of love, just me and her...
Oh black heaven is more than I deserve...

Them

I hate the way they sound…Them, those others
I hate how they love…Them, those lovers
I hate how they push…Them, those covers
I hate how I feel… Breathless demon hovers
Who touched my robe in my mind?
Who gave me this blood in my wine?
Let us go in those pigs, those pigs
These aren't lies, their fibs, their fibs
I want to drown in your ocean god
Cast the demons out of my coyote dog
The sin, the sin, made me go insane
I'm them, I'm them, make them go away

God of Blue

Drinking wine dark,

Tasty blueness of the deep sea

Blue lights, I shall call upon thee

Look at the moon in the dark blue night

Surrounded by baby blue in the sunrise sunlight

Color of truth, serenity and harmony

Shine your healing light upon me

Through the dark and through the fog

I found the favorite color of god

Look at mother earth through eyes of space

Her beautiful, beautiful romantic blue face

The beautiful spring blue sky of May

Sing us Scottish songs of blae

Blue light, blue light come out tonight

I once was blind but now I see

The blue of love has set me free

Icy howl and Icy blue

We write of the life we never knew

Oh god of blue

Day 6

One last promise my love,
they say unto death do we part,
but I will love you even in death...

I chose November thirteen that was the first time I saw you. That day I was drowning in your eyes of curiosity, and I floated in your waves of wonder. I know I left you, and I know I thought Kael was the one, but she was an accident, her green eyes under death's cold ice, even her death was an accident, but you were destiny. I doubted destiny. For that forgive me, please forgive me.

I have so much more to say,
but I'm running out of time.
I have that one more thing,
before I can do that one last thing I promised.

Blood Mountain

Why was there blood in the mountain that night?

The howl of the Cherokee...

The howl of the Creek Indians...

There was much blood; I thought it was a new stream.

The clouds vanished from the moon and the moonlight showed the mountain was covered in red...

You have come to push me, but we are not one...

We have fought dragons before; we have killed vampires and zombies...

Oh... But you dreamed of being a fallen angel...Now the fallen angel has come...

To the wrong woods, these are the woods of heaven...

I planted these trees;

I made this forest, and this mountain...

Haven't you heard the story of death

slithering in trees?

If I walk away do you believe you can deceive her again? She has no flesh yet...

I should have known you only made my mountain look like it was bleeding...

There has been no blood here since

the old earth died....

What is that you say?

Oh yes, I've heard there was lots of blood before the first earth was made...

Enough... You can't have my soul...

I won't leave being a pure human again...

How did you get here? You were turned into ashes…

You were turned into ashes in the fire of forever and ever…

You can't come here, you're not alive…

You can't come here and ruin my forest and paint my mountain red… Stop looking at her! She's my lover……My pure lover…….. She will not be deceived again….We saw the death of our world…

All of this is only thought and choice……..

I choose love this day forever…

It happened here on Blood Mountain…

You can't come here; we don't believe you this time…

We don't believe you're even alive…

I would say go away, but these thoughts are mine because you died on Blood Mountain and I will use your ashes in the new world to grow my trees…

This is my forest, my trees, my woods, here on Blood Mountain, and death is no more.

Night of Fire
Killed your Skelton closet
Pulled Phantasies out of your soul
Wrapped the clock around your neck
Sucked the new out of the old
I unsowed your eyes…So you can see me once again
I ate your disenchanted lie... Bloody number ten
I pumped your body with lemon as your sour bled
Bleeding down your yellowish grayish dark lips
Night of fire....... New imagination…
Oh sacred ghost... Phantom sensation…
Oh lovely ghost I could leave this day
Sit with thee in the moon away
It's okay… Said me, myself, and I
Was that the vampire Or my own mind?
I tried to forget the devil's dark…
By walking in the Halls of My gothic heart
Night of Fire
Night of fire
I found the new creature…
Born Again…

Wolf of Dark Love

I'm not the lion in the Bible,
nor a wolf in sheep clothing…
I have eaten foxes, coyotes, deer,
sheep and even other wolves
My favorite is sheep and fox meat
I've always slept during the day;
I didn't know what daylight was.
I did wonder how the moonlight was lit.
I heard it was the reflected yellow fiery stone in the sky.
I felt it burn my eyes.
I wondered who or what lit the yellow stone in the sky?
What's the chance of there being something that keeps
burning and shinning
Keeping us all alive…
Really, how strange…
Why yellow for the day…
Why dark for the night…
Why can't the evening stay…
Swallowed by the moonlight…
I'm I in this story…
Your golden glory…
I heard nothing by the midnight preacher…
Is my name found in scripture?
So I followed the wind…
To the Door within…
In this sacred book pictures

In-between versus, curses of scriptures…
Don't you see, don't you hear, the light above?
Reflecting Stonelight made you…Wolf of dark love…
So where I'm I? Did you seek & find…
The Stonelight & the Resurrection of Love
Did you find yourself…The new self
I'm not talking of the devil's darkness…
I'm not talking of any kind of evil…
I'm talking about the dark sacred love of Christ…
Dark Love howling for the prodigals to come home…
To the light of heaven where love is from…

Pale Light Kiss

(Lucian's Song of Songs #5)

The sacred hunter…
The king's daughters
Pulling me up from the widow
Holding me tight… Don't let go
Such a drunken delight…
With a glass of moonlight
All the knights have fallen
All the missed kisses from stalling
Purple….Cold purple lips
Pale light kiss
Invite me…Surprise me…
Oh story of all stories behind the door
Oh ecstasy's tears wanting more
Come swim with me in the river of life
Come taste the love that invented the night
I'm right here at your window
He's not dead but you're still a widow
Let me kiss your soft soul
With a pale light kiss…
Bring back your dreams…You still miss…
Wish again my love…..Wish…
Here in your window…Pale light kiss…

New Window

Have you been waiting
Anticipating
The new grand view…The new color blue
Science discovers love…Love past the sky above
Not like those gray days outside your dark window
Not like the woman who has become the lonely widow
There's something beautiful in the white shadow
The pale moonlight soft pillow
Looking out your new window
So this is what it was
They gave us our supernatural buzz
We guessed at what angels were
We wondered why pain so badly hurt
Death where is your sting?
We've become little children
with our voices we sing
Come, come, and look out your new window
Come, see this is what we've all big looking for
Open, open, open up the door
No more bad windows and no more crooked floors
New Window…. By Stonelight

Ghost of the Old World
Midnight moon and red scared tea
Me and my scarecrow sailing the black sea
The crisp dark shadowy blare
Zombie eyes stare & glare
Playing in the ocean killing God's whales
Tickling heaven's feet & shivering cold hells
The sun turned off its light
Right on time for the midnight fight
Ghost sailors... Sailing way
1,000 years the devil is all alone...
1,000 years snake breathes them bones...
Not I... not I... Throwing away the devil's eye...
Watching revelation's crystal ball
Watching the light angels fall
The Scarecrow burns its own straw...
The scarecrow comes to burn us all...
This was the story once upon a time
Before the earth & heaven's new wine
Before the trumpet sound
Before the fire came down
Ghost sailors... Sailing away
On this new ocean...
On this new day...
Ghost of the old world...
Sailing... Sailing away...

Escaping Asylum

Beautiful flowers and plum trees
Lights of New York City and bumble bees
Went to Edgar Allan Poe's grave
Saw C.S. Lewis just the other day
Not allowed to speak to the dead,
 But they speak to me
Aren't the dead supposed to leave us be
The pain runs deeper than the blood
Pass the bones into the broken soul of love
Lord I use to believe in you, do you still believe in me
Will your blood still cover if there nothing left of me
Soda pop, candy, t.v. lights, and more
I can hear the knocking but I can't answer the door...
escaping asylum
Kael is under the ice... kael my love...
That night on the lake became a dragon dove...
The pain so deep... A living hell
So I cast my wish in the dark wishing well...
Like Saints closing their eyes to come alive...
I'm folding my hands it's so dark inside...
escaping
escaping
escaping asylum

God of Darkness

Twilight…Moonlight…

The summer night's charcoal
Warming up my little lit soul
The other side of you
The wild in wolves howling heaven's blues
Turning water into wine
Watching the stars shine
In the darkness of night
You're not just the God of light
How did the sun know we needed to be awake?
How did the moon know we needed to sleep?
Where is the light in the ocean so deep?
You are the God of darkness
But not the dark that's heartless
The darkness of beauty
Night grace light of duty
When I close my eyes the darkness is yours
When I sleep the darkness is yours

Why does holiness hide in such dark places?
Why can't we see you till we have faces?

I'll awake where
there is no sun or moon but you the light thereof…
When I awake
 I will be in the light of your begotten love…

        God of Light… by Stonelight

Black Ghost
You drained me…Didn't understand me
Eyes rolled back…The dark you see
Not the same dark I see
Black Ghost…Black Ghost
The drugs we take to get rid of you
Rich man's blues
Guitar broken fingers bruised
That's not what I said
That's not what you read
Lime sour bled
Black Ghost…Black Ghost
The light we take to get rid of you
Give me gray…
dead ed gar al in my scotch of horrors..
I forgot all these doors of horrors
Just on the edge of darkness
Just one edge of light
Dull Gray,,,,,,,,,,
Haunted laughter in that day dull day
Shadows that aren't meant to be
gloomy hotels… Dark suppression...
All this to say....
Black Ghost…Go away!

Wilted
I'm watching myself die
Too busy to hear you cry
The blood so red
Icy River ahead
Zombie lover
No romance to discover
Feel the devil shiver
Down the wild river
And the flowers grew thorns
And the flowers bled
d…dyi…dying…
Wilted & Dead

Souls & Shadows
Can I come in?
Explore how wonderful you are…
Your spirit…Your ghost… I so love
white, pale, pink,
I spill my ink…
Shadow on soul…
Souls and Shadows…
Lost in wind…
Born again…
Tasty as plumbs…
In the pines of love…
If only, if only I could find you…
I just wanted to write my shadow on your soul…
Come on baby… Come on
Shadow on soul…
Fall…
Fall in love…
Souls & Shadows…

Dark Side of Genius

P a i n t i n g s of A s y l u m s

His last words "The sadness will last forever"
Somewhere in the field splattered blood
I found the gun, where the light angel won
evil never wants beauty to be fully painted
Don't remind them of life before love was tainted
I feel you in the back woods of heaven's trails
The voices of heavens and forgotten hells
self-portraits, wheat fields, and sunflowers
Painting your way out of asylum's dark powers
Sitting at Dr. Gachet red table talking romantic theater
Conversations of life and potato eaters
There's a crack in the universe where all spirits slip away
Your bullet in my soul and the day by day
You brushed my life and didn't even know my name
1,900 paintings and you hardly sold thing…
Dark poets die young, and become little queens & kings…
Give him a proper funeral you heartless, oh ye heartless
Look at all the light and love, even in darkness…
We are yellow wheat fields and dark crows
Love and to Love…Is All we should ever know.
In these paintings of asylums, our last golden show

P a i n t i n g s of A s y l u m s……
(Dark Poets Die Young #15)

In the Death of Love

It was a sick game we played
Picking the ways we'd die
Once a year
One of us would kiss the sky

Some kind of dark magic
We didn't believe in
We found our fallen code
In the devil's deep sin

Kissing the lips of darkness
No… it wasn't, it was the white shadow
In my heart, the dark hollow

They forget how dark
Sweet smiles & decoys
 Vampires & tree toys

And over and over
 The winds would cry

In the moonless dark
We said it 3 times

Blood & Love

We saw ourselves
We saw who we are
In the death of love

We saw them
We saw us
In the death of love

On Sex Mountain (Lucian's Song of Songs)

I'm chasing you... Yeah the wolf is coming
I fast now... Yeah in loving
You're panting, but not enough
You're still breathing with red lust
The moon is about...
Silver gray on the lookout...
Our love will burn this forest down...
Sparks of life... sparks of passion
devil watching lonely as we're laughing...
Silver bullets swooshing by
We don't care... Love is high...
splashing in rivers, cold, and sexy shivers
The whole mountain is shaking
The Volcano is about to erupt
Live and love.... Some call it luck
Oh jealous... Oh jealous moon...
Looking so Pale...
My baby and I down all the rabbit trails
Lucian Wilde and my sweet Kael...

Soul Burns

10, 000 years ago I felt your pain
 In these nights of tears and rain
I can't find the night tonight
No stars fallen from the sky
Like magical evolution
The wind brought me to life
In The Dark Side of Genius
Shaky nervous twitch
Not easy to live with
Dark delusion
Midnight conclusion
Poetry, passion, and dying bones
World filled with people, I still feel alone
Can't walk a straight line
Twisted turns and dark wine
Making electricity out gray clouds
Intuitionism speaking loud
Here in the Dark Side of Genius
How much she really loved me
No matter how learned
I could never earn
Her love and these soul burns

The Dark Side of Genius #2

(Roses & Thorns)

Lucifer are you lonely like me
Are you in death like me
Unfree like me
Lucifer are you cold indeed
In a place of unbelief
What do you think of the color pink
or Lucian Wilde's poetry dark ink
When's the last time you smiled
When's the last time you had a good memory
Why was heaven hell
Why is hell heaven
Why number six and not seven
Lucifer why did change you name
So filled with shame
Roses and thorns
Devils and horns
All die and return to the ground
Until the trumpet sound
I'll be gone and undead
You'll still be dead
Just dead instead
Not like me...
No more horns
I'll be a rose
With no more thorns...

The Dark Side of Genius #3

(Dark Mist)

In these dark waters
In this forest of fog
"Am I all alone…"
Says God
Just me projecting
It's just me protecting
The wind kisses me
The water becomes life
I drink… I sink
These thoughts I think
Glaring off the dark edge
Yesterday I was like dead
I didn't exist
Now with your kiss
I see the light
In the stars of the night
Dark Mist
Dark Kiss
And you love me
But now I must say good bye
We die…… we all die
You never wanted this…
I know I did this
One day I'll be with you again
The spirit hovered over the waters
The spirit hovers
Covers…
Like Sacred Lovers…

The Dark Side of Genius # 4

(Thousand Dark Skies)

I open my eyes
To another dark sky
Ocean too deep
Stormy waves can't sleep
But I still want
I still want love
These dungeon eyes
A thousand dark skies
Telling me to sleep forever
Devil fox so clever
Blurry days can't pray
The black ghost comes to play
Am I sick, I don't feel so good
Do you smell death; burnt wood
I can't see… I can't feel.
Only a dark chill
Those vampires' lies
Listen to their cries
The killing of an evil heart
For more bright days in the dark
Or just one bright day in the night….
Face to face with the maker
The maker of light
In a thousand dark skies
 Baptizing me in a thousand dark skies…

The Dark Side of Genius # 5

(Song of the Scarecrow)

Evil in the name of peace ... White shadows teach
Blood and bleach ...Alluring love smiling bewitched
Gospel of death devils twitch ... Into your kissy bloody lips
Bottomless hips...Hell sells and death dwells
Cheap dark smoke...Creepy fingers poke
Black birds pray for fire
Watching leaves fall off with a holy flashlight
Counting stars, soaking in the pale of midnight

Scarecrows sing the song of the crow

"We know the dark bird will eat us, we taste it in our blood.
Oh vampire, Geist of imagination, we thought to death,
and evil came into the mind of an angel... And evil came
into the mind of us all...
Seeing our faces on the dark side of the cross with the light
on the other side... The Dark side of Genius comes to haunt
us like hounds of heaven..."

Crows sings the song of the scarecrow

"Dark matter, dark ladder, spoil light scatters...
They're not afraid of the maker of dark feathers...
Our dark wings...They're not afraid of the seed giving
birth in the soil...
Oh but they eat, they eat all your food...
The laugh in your face and call you no good...
They eat and eat all your food
Laugh and mock and call you no good...

The Templin Ghost Story
(Is there a ghost at the Red Lion Hotel?)

Some say so, though the short story/poem "Haunted Piano" is not based a ghost story. The novelist, who wrote the book "Green Eyes on Ice", "Dark Wishing Well, and "Lost Vampire Letters" says "It's not based on a ghost story, but on a unfinished love story that would self-destructs in a romantic suicidal poetic way …"

One day walking down the hallway at the Red Lion Hotel, he says he felt a strange vibe or a strange presence of some sort walking by a piano. Not sure of what it was, he decided to write "The Haunted Piano." Not long after that other employees admitted of feeling that same awkwardness when walking by the Piano at the Red Lion in Post Falls.
So is there a Red Lion ghost?

It's been said there was a man who unexpectedly died in his sleep at the Red Lion. But that's not so odd; people do die in their sleep. Investigating the story a little further and some say they saw him playing the piano the day before.

The second possibility was an accident that took a few construction workers' lives while working on the hotel's second floor, which had no walls yet. The rushing wind came down the mountain, across the river, and up the hillside like a vortex and sent the workers soaring to their deaths. The place where is the wind had lifted them off the ground is where the Red Lion's piano is placed. Out of the three main stories, this one seems to give some Red Lion employees the eeriest feeling.

The third story is Red Lion had a small two story white house that was torn down on their corner lot property. The white house was torn down because it was old, decaying, and unlivable. Unlivable for whom? Further investigating the story we discovered there was a dark poet in the late 70's or early1980's who lived in the house shot himself as he was playing the piano. Why did he shoot himself? It was reported that his mistress had killed herself in the river behind The Post Falls Red Lion Resort. After killing himself it was said the Mistress would come and play the Piano at night according to the neighbors. Now that the house is torn down and gone, and since it was Red Lion's house, some would suggest that her ghost now comes and plays the Piano at the Red Lion Hotel. Others suggest it might be the man who shot himself playing for his mistress because she drowned in the river. Since there are two pianos at the Red Lion, could it be a ghostly duet…

"Haunted Piano" is not based on a ghost story or is it?

The Haunted Piano

He enters the old Victorian hotel at midnight, and walks down the hall, and down the stairs. When he gets to the bottom of the stairs he feels an off presence down the hall to the left of him. He opens the door, to a dark bluish room, and in the corner he spots an old piano. He looks around and sees no one. "Oh…"He thinks to himself, "Why not", but every step closer to the piano he feels the off presence getting stronger. He almost feels like he's doing something wrong. "I think I should just go to bed, maybe another night", and so he walks away…

As he lies in bed he feels betrayal, cold feet, and sweaty hands. He thought of the Piano, and the strange feeling. Stressed and anxiety was setting in. "Get up, and just play it…" "Fine", he thought, "I'll just play it!"

He started walking across the hall, when he thought, "This is ridiculous, I have a piano at home…" "Stop thinking and play!"…… "Wait, that wasn't my voice!" "Stop thinking and play, and when you're done kill him!" "Kill who and who are you?"

"I am the piano, play me, I'll put lyrics in your mind, and you'll know what to do…"

Haunted Piano (Act 1)

(Give Her Away)

"Give her away
Some other day
You can love her again
But not this time
Drink some wine
Say it okay
Here's a rope or a gun
Moon and fun
Love and young
Bullet will rush it all away
Time to go
One last prayer to pray
"But I love her"
"You can't... Not this time..."

Haunted Piano (Act 2)

(Playing for the Dead)

I don't want to sing this
You and your poison kiss
"But it's your words!!"
Music you've never heard
It's okay its safe here
No more tears
"I just want to sing her a love song"
"As your last word?"
What last words?
"Why are you so selfish? Just sing her the song…"
I can't
I can't feel
I can't steal
She so real
My only desire
My warm camp fire
A dream of all dreams
Need of all needs
But not here… not now
Past the clouds somehow
"Then hear take the rope and just do it…"
"Do what?"
"Okay, but let me sing her my song"
"Fine! but she'll never hear it…"

Haunted Piano (Act 3)

(The End)

I saw you there
I saw you stare
I never saw love before
I couldn't believe
What I could see
Behind the forgotten door
Will you be mine
Make this heart shine
Heaven is kissing me
Your soul sets me free
If only we could be together
Hopefully in forever
I love you…

………..I………..Love……………..You…

The maid comes in and screams… "There's blood on the piano, there's blood on the piano!!"
But there was no body to be found…

Haunted Piano (Act 4)

(Where's My Lover)

She had a strange feeling that night. Something was wrong, and she hadn't heard from him in days. "That's not like him; he talks to me every night", the thought out loud... She knew he was nearly impossible to love, but she had to try. She loved his dark poetic ways and his drunken humor. He seemed like he could love, the rumor was he loved everyone in some sort of way. It was the dark cracks of hearts that some fell in. She loved him and no matter how many times she fell in, she was always able to climb out, but this time he's gone. She hadn't heard a word.

She packed her bags to go visit the last hotel he stayed at, and when she got there she was horrified by the news. "This was where the maid was when she screamed. "There's blood on the piano, there's blood on the piano!!" But there was no body to be found... "Was there blood?" "No", said the manager of the hotel, "There was no body or blood, just the old piano that the maid said had blood on it. But it true your dark poet is gone, and he never checked out, and he's always checks out."
    With tears In her eyes, "Yes... Yes, and he's calls my every night. Something is wrong, I can just feel it. May I have some time to just sit here by this piano?" "Oh, of course, and take your time." She had a really bad feeling that he was really gone. To where and how and why she didn't know, all she knew is she wanted to play this old piano and write him a song. She slowly put her hands on the keys, and softly pressed down and began to sing...

Haunted Piano (Act 5)
(Mistress No More)

"I knew this day would come
My whole world undone
I knew this day would come
I just tried not to believe
Oh… How I love you
I have no choice but to live alone
You taught how to be a lady
You taught me how to be Wilde
When you have to say good bye,
those good byes hurt the most
Your somewhere…….A ghost
Oh dark poet thank you for the love we shared
 Now a mistress no more
I had to close the door
If you're not dead, you would be proud of me
I've decided to live on, and be free
But I'll always love you
Yes… I'll always love you
Good bye dark poet
Good bye…
I'm a mistress no more…
She didn't feel the blood dripping off the piano
 onto her feet.
The piano wasn't bleeding.
The piano wasn't haunted.
The poet died of a broken heart
 His heart bled to death
No one wants to say good bye…
We all do in this life…
 We all become life's mistress no more…

Not Dark Enough

The dream of a clown
 In blood you drown
 Not dark enough

Snake slithers in your mouth
 Stranger sitting on your couch
 Not dark enough

Demons screaming in hell
 Your mind, a twisted cell
 Still not dark enough

Edgar Allan Poe speaks in one ear
 Oscar Wilde in the other
 Very dark, still not dark enough

The door knob slowly turning
 Your spirit begins burning
 A dark eeriness begins…

Your tumbling soul is discerning
 You hear a voice that's concerning
 And the dark eeriness comes in…

"I hear the voices", she says"----"What do they say?"
 "They're crying", she says--- "What are they crying for?"

Lucian…. Lucian… Is that you?
 "I hear the Sun crashing into the moon…"

DARK HOUSE OF WOODS 123 (Part 2)

I felt the moon pull the tide
I felt my spirit come alive
Walking past house 125
Through the woods and twisted trees
Dark woods of 123
Every time I stare, stunned
Don't know if I should stare or run
Spirit artist of the sky
The devil on the corner in disguise
Good and evil are not equal
Just enough for another poem sequel
Life in color and black and white pictures
The devil man tries to ditch her
Believe; believe, if you can believe
All this in the dark house of woods 123
July crashes with august sky
Feel the moon pull inside
Spirit's eye wandering tide
Windy trees and fairy tales
Darkness and icy hells
All undone with a holy whisper
The kiss of lips
That will never ditch her
Believe; believe, if you can believe
All this in the dark house of woods 123

Dark Hymn of Light

Lonely for holy
Not for flesh
Lonely for spirit
No longer possessed…
So this is what it feels like to take off the devil's horn
So this is what it feels like to be reborn

Lonely for holy
Not for flesh
Lonely for spirit
Till my last breath…
So this is what it feels like when mystery wind blows
So this is what feels like to be in the sacred show

Lonely for holy
Not for flesh
Lonely for spirit
There's life in death…
So this is what feels like to praise the maker of night
So this is what feels like to sing the dark hymn of light…

Dark Hymn of Light #2

(Tree of Color)

Once I saw you green and alive
Now your pine needles became fallen goodbyes
Breathless cold... No longer alive
Whatever happened to green living
Now red and bleeding
Lifeless, fearful, unbelieving
Then Christmas came
Came in every color
Boys and girls laughed joyfully with each other
We saw green like spring
Red bride of roses and the royal king
Death no longer my Eve the queen
We sang,
"The tree is green again...
A resurrection of green again...
Full of colors and believing again...
Full of love and seeing again...
We wish, we wish, you the tree of color...
Every son and every daughter...
We wish you a merry merry tree of color...
Every son and every daughter..."
Tree of Color....

Dark Hymn of Light #4

(The Walking Dead)

Leftovers of evil
Lil d's of devils
Windy spiritual weather
Invisible souls & feathers
Written in the dark book of light
We read about the silent night

There
There it is

White wool
Blood wool
Dark wool

Hope died & fled
The Universe........ The walking dead

Then
There we saw

The grave stone became the stonelight
The walking dead... Begin a new life

Dark Hymn of Light #4
(The Walking Dead).......By Lucian Wilde

The Dark Side of Genius # 13

(The Other Way)

I saw the light and I wondered, but dark was home for me
To cross the line my heart was a forest, abatis...
The darkness cried when the sun came up!
But I felt...
I felt a holy bacchanal to the voice that wasn't cad like the plundering world
I felt instinct in a higher form, the voice was a lovely song singing "da capo is where you belong!
You have changed the music, the spirits, and the heart, come back to the beginning."
So I turned just a bit, knowing the turn was my choice, but not my will only.
A thousand angelic atmospheres shouted, "Come.... The other way, and breathe unspoiled air, and live forever!"
"What about this haunted train and dark alley stations I've known all my life? Ghost towns and shadows of the other lives I've lived?"
The voice came again, "Do you know how to make dark red in blood or the dark luscious red in wine?
"No I've, I've only drank it." "Yes, like the whole world it drinks not knowing what life really is, they've had a little taste, and propose a toast to the whole world saying, "We have seen and taste it all! We're all knowing! All religious monsters are dead, and all superstition is no longer, we've become love unto ourselves..."
"...They..." and it sounded like many voices, "Are closing the door of forever!"

Act 1
(Closing the Forever Door)

I heard the laughter in the ring
The demons come to sing
We no longer care
We do the god eye stare
Dark blood with black tongues
Black bullets with white guns
Shooting the moon away
Blocking the sun away
Forever……….. Foreverlightless
Forever……….. Foreverlightless
Careful what you wish for
When you close the forever door
Careful what you wish for
When you say you don't want more…

(To be continued) The Other Way….

Dark Hymn of Light #5

(Death of a Spirit)

Cloudless blue
Loving you
Leaves of every color
Sweet Smell of lovers

Cold and warm rivers
Lil sexy shivers
All in a touch
It's all we could ever want

Then evil came in the wind
We sang the songs of darkness
Losing our reflection in mirrors

"Oh death of a spirit
Oh death of our spirit"

Hiding all from what is good
Like the first day to the seventh
For a time
Love was all there was

Dark Hymn of Light # 9

(This Scared Night)

the spirit of the wind in the breeze
the spirit of love indeed
the spirit of a candle in need

In the flames... in flames the spirit has spoken
It has kept us warm in its orange token
Worship the spirit the unbroken

Live again no matter the shattered heart
Live again no matter how dark the dark

Be born of the spirit of life
Be born of the spirit of light
Be born again this sacred night

Into the world we see darkly
Into the world we see hardly
Into the world we live barely

Breathe This Sacred Night...

One Dark Day

**Immortal Beloved
Lost in my head
One Dark Day
Watch for the dead
I turned the cross upside down
Washed your blood off the devil's ground
You want me to pray, I can't pray
On this dark day
You smiled awkward
 Frowning backwards
Pretend lover
Under the cover
The wolf and its prey
On this one dark day
Drinking blood and scotch
Staring at the upside down cross
We all have the devil to pay
On this
One Dark Day…**

The Darkest of Lights

She's picking rotten strawberries of the field

He's a loving warrior without a shield

And the devils laugh, "You're no longer who you are…"

The government has taken over the world

We've become its slave every boy and girl

Where every wrong has been made right

They sing, "Is there still hope in the darkest of lights…"

I'd rather have worms in my apples

To be free and live in disaster

Mother earth is being raped by greedy liars

We're like hobbits longing for the shire

The blood of Abel screams from the ground

Now the unnatural circus is ruling our town

Is there a place where love can still be found?
I suppose when angels make the trumpet sound
Where everyone wrong will be made right
Here in the darkest, the darkest of lights…

All Is Dark

Such a dark thirst
Your drunken soul burst
Drinking the dark heart of Poe
In the dark wind that blows
I see… I see Redless
Your blue veins around your necklace
Oh poor baby
My dark lady
I made you pale like me…
Dark inside like me…
A story like me…
Sunless…Lightless … Like me
"Love is blindness
  I don't want to see
  Won't you wrap the night around me
  Oh my love…. Love is blindness…"
  All….is…. Dark

The Whisper of Love

It's not the wrong words
But the right words
It's not just the blood or the dark cross
Afraid of deep woods and being lost

Whisper Love
Just breezing by
Spirit Love
Tears and eyes
Whisper Love
 Love inside

It's not just the blood or the dark cross
Afraid of deep woods and being lost
It's us never knowing, until you hear
The Whisper of Love, loud and clear

The Whisper of Love

Dark Woods of House 123 (Part 3)
(Once Upon a Time Became Forever)

Pondering the dark side of genius
Faces of evil envious
The dark woods and the Lullaby tree
Surrounding house of 123
Next to Hankle, Hinkle, and Tummy Rub Rue
Carving out the piano no Princess' blues
Callie comes from the Castle of Wickum
Named after the wizard l o n g before them
You can hear the waves crashing inside my heart
In a place lit-filled with beautiful dark
Once upon a time became forever
Here in oceans forest, a calm surrender
Enter the twilight grayish doors
Kids are dancing & night creatures eating smores
Singing Halleluiah begging heaven for more
Listening to the sand tell our stories on the shore
Mixture of heat and cool sea breeze
Hemingway and I, and the old man and the sea
We're alive in the Dark Woods……. Of house 123...

Day 7

When you find this letter, I wasn't able to put in our keep sake box under our tattooed tree. I'm not able to walk through the forest right now. Like I told you, I have one last thing I need to do, and when I'm done, My blood will be yours, I will fly to you with no wings, no wires, and my blood will be yours, and we'll never be roses trampled on again. We will be like kites with no strings, there is one more bridge for us to cross, but you just lie still, I will carry you across. Only be ready to take my blood, together, forever, my sweet Eve. I'm going to crumble this paper up, and we'll face to face without words... I keep hearing this voice, these words in my head, like a strange dream; the sky falling apart, lighting, and a voice like a trumpet of victory, and I wake up saying your name... No, I'll save this letter, and you can read at the cabin soon, and you crumble it up, and know my love is more than words, more than the poetry I left for you to read in our secret place...

Brighter than the moon my sweet Eve;

always... Always...

Love, Lucian.

Red Chair in the Forest
(Earth's First Love)

Red chair in the forest
to remind all creatures that I'm the poet king
Birds take flight with cheerful songs they sing
In and out of the trees and flying around my throne
Letting me know the dark poet is never alone
It's a good day here in the woods, where life began
Away from the city air, yes where life began
the sounds of the river, like blood flowing in my veins
We never love, we never love in vain...
The world is dark with an evil dark
The world is dark with a good dark
Here I baptize my imagination in the darkness of good
Where holiness is brighter
than the light that's understood
Come sit with me here in these sacred woods
Bring a red chair, and be a king and queen with me
In the garden of Eden where a tree bleeds for thee
Red love and red chairs
with lungs full of moonlight above
Romance and kisses, all is welcomed, please come
Bring your red chair and
watch the world come undone
Bring a red chair and listen to the earth's first love...

Red Chair in the Forest... (Earth's First Love)

The Ling Low
(Why Children should never talk to strangers)

It was a nice sunny day with a few clouds and a cool breeze. Kids were playing soccer, flying kites, and some were playing tag. Other kids were watching a peculiar man showing them magic tricks. He was so funny with his knock, knock jokes.

Knock Knock.
Who's there? Lettuce. Lettuce Who? Lettuce in! it's cold out here!

Knock Knock.
Who's there? Boo. Boo Who? Awww, don't cry, it's just a joke!

They laughed and laughed. They also liked his white hat, and his friendly smile. It was like he knew a lot about life and in some ways it was like he knew everything....Even the parent enjoyed the interesting man.

The sun was slowly going down and the Mister was the first to leave the park. Some of the kids wanted to follow him home. He told the kids that he lived down the road a little ways. Some yelled out "will we ever see you again Mister?" "Maybe so", the Mister said, "Now you better go home with your parents and of course you know you should never talk to strangers unless your parents say okay. Bedsides, it's getting dark out, and the moonlight makes me tired."

The next day came and it was another beautiful day. The kids couldn't wait to go play at the park. They looked around for the Mister, and each kid was hoping to be the first kid to find him. But this time the Mister was no where to be found. A few days and then a few weeks went by, and still there was no Mister to be found.

The White Hat

The White Hat

One day one of the kids named Charlie from the neighborhood spotted the Mister and went to tell his sister Sarah and others on the block that he had seen the funny guy from the park. All the kids went looking for him. Nobody found him and the kids thought Charlie was just fooling.

Charlie was sad and disappointed until he came home and found the Mister's white hat on the front lawn. He picked it up and ran up to room and put the white hat on. It was a little big, but it was still fun to wear the Mister's hat. Charlie looked at his self in the mirror and started acting like he was the Mister. He didn't know someone was watching him through the crack of the door. All of a sudden he heard his little sister Sarah laughing. Charlie opened the door and yelled at her and asked "how long have you been watching me?" Sarah laughed, "Ever since I saw you running in the house like a bee was chasing you!" She started to laugh again. "Why were you running so fast? I saw you acting like that Mister we saw at the park… Why did you take his hat?" "I didn't, I found it on our front lawn. I wanna give it back to him as soon as possible!" "Really… I've seen him a few times myself." "When did you see him?" "When I heard him knocking at the door, I saw him outside my window." "No you didn't", Charlie said surprised! "Did you talk to him, did you let him in?" **knock, knock,** "what was that?" "It's someone knocking on the front door silly. Ha-ha it's probably the Mister now!"

Charlie and Sarah's mother opened the door, but it wasn't the Mister. It was the neighbor next door in distressed. "Hello can I help you?" "Yes, yes please!" She said nervously. "I can't find my boy James, have you seen him? Please tell me you have! "No I haven't seen little James, I'm sorry can we will help you look for him?" "Yes please help me look for him!" A sick feeling came over the distressed woman, like a snake had just slithered over her bare feet. For weeks the police and neighbors looked for little James and never found him. She remembered her son talking about a new fishing spot that some stranger told him about. The stranger told James, "It's the biggest fish you ever saw." And that was the last conversation she had with her son. The mother cried and feared she would never see her boy again and shouted, "I told that boy to never talk to strangers,

"I told him a hundred times and now he's gone and I will never see him again. And sure enough that was the last time anybody ever saw little James.

Another week went by and another child was missing. It was horrible like out of scary movie. Children we're disappearing. For a while kids were not allowed to play outside even on a warm and beautiful day. It took two months before kids started slowly coming out of their houses again. It was like a month of rain and thunder and lighting. The truth is it only rained once and the only thunder was pain in the hearts of parents whose children were still missing. Unfortunately no matter how many times parents tell their kids not to talk to strangers, there's always that one that still doesn't listen.

Didn't Your Parents Tell You Not To Talk To Strangers!

Charlie was a nice boy; he was smart and so was his sister Sarah. They both loved each other very much. They went for walks and played together all the time. Today was one of those days they went for a walk. On their walk they saw the Mister. "Yay finally…!" They waved and yelled, "Hey Mister!" They yelled and yelled, but the Mister couldn't hear them even though they weren't far away. "Strange", thought Charlie. "Why can't he hear us?" "Hey Mister", they yelled again and the Mister still kept on walking up to the porch of his house. He looked around as if he heard some one calling his name and then finally he walked into his house. "Is that the Mister's house?" Sarah asked.
"I don't know!" said Charlie, "If it is we can return his hat. Quick lets run home and get his hat."

Charlie and Sarah were so excited to bring that Mister's hat back. So excited, they didn't even tell their mother or father where they were going. They ran in and they ran out like lightning bolts. They ran back to the Mister's house that was just a few blocks over. The house was beautiful with a marvelous front yard. Charlie said "have you ever seen such an awesome place"? "No, I haven't, it's wonderful…"

They started walking toward the house; they started to feel strange like maybe they should tell their parents where they were. They were just about to leave, when they heard laughter. The laughing was so funny; they remembered how funny the Mister was at the park. His laughter was so funny they started laughing too. "Come on", said Charlie. We're here now, mise well give the Mister's hat back." So they went up to the door and started to knock and soon as they did the door opened, and there he was. "Hey kids what can I do for you? Hey! You found my hat, you found my hat!" "Come in, come in, I've been looking for that hat for days."

"I'm glad you kids are here I want to show you something." The Mister rolled up his sleeves and started to show Charlie and Sarah a new trick he was learning. The Mister took a piece of paper and made it into a paper air plane and then threw it into the air and as it was floating it turned into a butterfly and flew out the window. "Wow", shouted Charlie and Sarah. "Do it again, do it again!" "Okay, but first let me show you something else. Can you smell that? I made you the best cookies you'll ever have. Have
you ever heard of Narnia?" "Oh yes we have!" "Oh wonderful, well wait right here on the couch,
I made something special for you."

Charlie and Sarah couldn't wait. But at the same time they had strange feeling come over them again like they should go home and tell their parents where they were. Charlie was looking over at where the Mister hung his hat and thought it was odd to see six other hats that all looked exactly alike. The kitchen door swung open and the Mister had a big smile and had a tray full of cookies. "I named these cookies after the Narnia's cookies; I call them Ling lows delight, try some!" "Yum, oh yum, oh these are the best cookies we've ever had."

"What's your favorite part in the story of Narnia?" "Well let me think Charlie." He thought for a moment, "I think I liked how it was always winter, but never Christmas." Sarah had thought that was really strange, but what was bugging Charlie was all those white hats on the wall. "Mister, why do you have all those hats, they all look alike?" "Well replied the Mister, you see I loose my hats all the time." Then he mumbled quietly, "**Some just don't bring them back**!"

"What do you do," asked Sarah. The Mister thought for a while making her feel awkward for asking "What do I do?" The Mister started acting stranger and stranger with ever question. Charlie and Sarah were started to feel bit nervous and bit scared, but they were trying not to show it. The Mister replied "I'm a writer". "What's your favorite story you have written so far?" You could hear the nervousness in Sarah's voice. The Mister Quickly responding with a smile, flying out of cat's Ville, the Mister laughed with a creepy laugh "The cat that wanted to fly, the children just love that one."

Charlie was thinking of something to say so they could leave, but Sarah asked another question. "Sir why do you call your cookies the ling low delights, and what's a ling low?" With a sarcastic creepy voice, the Mister responded "didn't your parents ever tell you that you shouldn't talk to strangers?" The Misters voice changed with a scary evil tone. "A Ling Low sucks the blood out of children's hearts!" And right then his smile showed two wolf like teethe that shot out into the heart of Charlie and Sarah, a tooth in each heart. The Mister started to flash and drink…

The flashing hypnotize them with fear as the blood was being sucked our out their little bodies. They could see his dark heart with every flash. They cried out, but nobody could hear their little screams…Nobody ever saw Charlie and Sarah again, and nobody found The Ling Low. That horrible day creature pretending to be so friendly and yet so deceiving….Poor Charlie and Sarah, they didn't ask their parents or tell them where they were going.

Never Answer the Door without Your Parents

Years went by and there was a new family that moved in. Who knows maybe just down the block from where you live. The new kids on the block where very nice children. Their names were Seth and Bella. Seth was nine and Bella was five and they loved each other so much. They played and went everywhere together. It's really neat to see a brother and sister who care so much for each other. I'm sure their dad and mom are super proud of them.

One day Bella was looking for her cat, but Mr. Cuddles was nowhere to be found.
All day they looked for cat and soon it was no longer light outside. Bella thought maybe Mr. Cuddles ran away. Seth and Bella looked for three more days for Mr. Cuddles, and still Mr. Cuddles didn't come home. Bella was sad.

On the fourth day Seth and Bella got up and looked out side and it was beautiful day. **Knock, knock**… There was a knock at the door. *"I wonder who's here"*, thought Bella. Running down the stairs to answer the door and right when she was about to answer Bella's mother yelled out, "Don't answer that door! Wait till I come down and see who it is. Little people she never answer the door on their own."

There was a knock again, "hold on", Bella said. My momma is coming, she'll be right here…" "Oh…good girl for waiting Bella", mother said as she opened the door. "Can I help you?" It was a young lady with a pretty pink dress. "Yes" she said, "is this your cat?" with a friendly concerned voice. "This cat keeps coming over to my yard, and walks inside my house and I found it asleep under my bed today. I've been knocking on every door hoping to find its home" "Oh …yes, yes, it is, and thank you so much!"

Bella was so happy; she grabbed Mr. Cuddles from the lady's hands and gave it a big hug. "It feels like you've been gone forever Mr. Cuddles." Bella's mother was so happy and asked the lady where she lived? She smiled and said "Oh, not far, I just live right around the corner." "Oh… well that's wonderful and thanks again. The kids have been looking for days now."

"Oh you're so welcome", as she patted Mr. Cuddles on the head. "Your welcome to little one." The lady smiled, turned, and walked away. "Wow mama, what a nice lady and she has such a pretty pink dress mama." "Yes dear, it sure was pretty, and it was kind of her to bring Mr. Cuddles home to us."

Scary News Report

"Time for bed…"Seth and Bella's parents kiss them and tucked them into bed.
Then went down stairs and turned the T.V. on only to see some awful news and the headlines was,
"The Ling Low has struck again!"

"This is the eleven O'clock news with a special report to let you know what a Ling Low is." Dad turned the volume up… "A Ling Low from the outside looks like any one of us! It can look like an old man, young woman, skinny, fat, small or tall, nice person or scary person. It can look friendly, grumpy, white, black, red, and yellow or any color. A Ling Low could look like anybody. It can even look like somebody you know…A Ling Low can sound like the nicest person you've ever met.

A Ling Low looks like us, but it's not. Its heart has become black as coal. You might have read stories about scary creatures of the night like vampires, but The Ling Low is a creature of the day. It is the opposite of scary night creature; The Ling Low is powerful in the day and is weak at night. It tries to lure your children with its very friendly smile.

The best stories could be coming from a Ling Low. They're great story tellers, but their goal is lure your children away. If it succeeds, you most likely will never see your kids again. We hate to scare parents like this, but that's what keeps Ling Lows alive is the fresh blood of little children. So again please tell your children never to talk to stranger!

The Ling low will suck your blood out with deadly wolf like vampire fangs. The Ling Low's teeth are at the bottom of their mouth. They don't bite you with them, their teeth shoot out of their mouth and it sticks into your heart. They suck the blood out of your heart with rubber tubes that comes out of their mouth attached to their teeth.

At this point if you're hearing this story for the first time let us remind you and we hope this makes you feel better so everyone sleep well tonight. The Ling Low rarely attacks at night, mostly in the day time, but they do steal cats and small dogs at night. Then they'll try to give them back a few days later so you will like and trust them.

The Ling Low is filled with a horrible darkness, and is no longer a normal person. That's why the Ling Low doesn't like the night; the only darkness it wants to see is itself. No dark competition allowed and so The Ling Low sleeps mostly at nights waiting for the moon to go away. When it drinks blood, the Ling Low's body flashes, kind of like turning a light switch off and on as fast as you can. Light, flash, dark, light, flash, dark, and it causes you to feel dizzy. You see them as normal person, but when they flash you see through their skin their dark heart within…

Another Alert
Just came in another alert …Two Ling Lows have recently been spotted. One is a man wearing a white hat; the other is a lady wearing a pretty pink dress, acting like she found your cat. Please keep look out and keep your kids safe…

After hearing that scary news report the father and mother turned the T.V. off and went and looked at Seth and Bella sleeping in their beds. "Oh good their sound asleep…" Later on that night, the father heard a noise. So he got up to check on Seth and Bella. Seth was sound asleep with his room light still on. He flicked the light switch off and whispered, "Good Night Son." Then he looked in Bella's room. Bella wasn't there. "Bella, where are you?" He didn't hear anything. He looked under bed and in the closet, and still no Bella. "Where is she?" He hurriedly walked down the stairs. Getting more and more nervous, thinking of the worse, but then he saw her. "Oh phew, there you are! What are you doing up little Missy?"

"Hi daddy,
I was watching the lady
in the pretty prink dress pet Mr. Cuddles."

End of Illusion

Song of Songs 8:6-7

It was rumored that the next show would be Auralia's last. Even though some would say she was the "finest Illusionist", her beauty over-shadowed her art, her talent, in the eyes of them, her fans, her watchers….

They always demanded that one more thing from her, and that one more thing was the true magic she refused to share with anyone. "How much magic should I perform for these vultures? Where, oh where, are those kind birds chirping outside my windows?" Of course she knew not even birds sang at night… "Sleeping beauty by day and vampires bats by night…"

No one bothered to ask her if it really was her last show… She cried that night, and felt like Moses striking the rock… "My promised land is a place where I am loved for who, not what, I am..." She could not wait to show them her main act tomorrow night. "If they love my art more than my beauty", she thought, "I will continue to be their enchanting illusionist."

Blaine had also heard the rumor. He was saddened that he had not told her how he felt. He thought, "Tonight will be the night!" He practiced looking in the mirror of what he would say... "Auralia I have been watching your shows and I have read your stories and articles. I love the WAY you are. I know everyone has seen how beautiful you are, and by all means you are stunning, more than eyes can take in... But who you are as a person is even more beautiful..." He practiced it a few more times in the mirror. "Would you consider going out on a date with me? I want to know more of who you." Satisfied with his little presentation, he tried to sleep for the morning of the big night was twenty hours away and counting.

"Tickets please!" *"Ah, the big night has come."* He handed in his ticket and waited for the wonderful sound of the ticket being ripped in half. "I've kept all 17 ticket stubs", he told the ticket taker with excitement. The man smiled and said, "Your seat is down the middle near the front" "Thank You." Quickly he made his way down.

The theater lights dimmed, a soft violin began to play, and the red curtains slid open with a grand swoosh. There she was walking across the stage in a blue silvery dress. She walked with such elegance, and when she spoke, he listened closely to her every word, as if his very life depended on it. "Tonight I have a new act that no one has ever seen before. I'm sure you'll wonder how I did this one." After forty five minutes of doing her best to please the audience, she could see the look in their eyes. It wasn't enough... Frustrated! She felt like making herself disappear, and not show them the fullness of what she could do. "I will do it anyway... There's no way they will be able to deny power over beauty."

Before Auralia did her final act she decided to say something that reflected how she felt. "There's nothing wrong with beauty, for beauty is a gift and lovely, but to only love someone for their beauty is not enough. A person has to be loved for more." She continued and only a few minutes later she realized it was useless. Their eyes gave her their answers.

But Blaine was nothing like the others, he wanted all of her... "How did she make the ceiling part ways?"

She reached for the moon like she was pulling an invisible string. "Under your seat there are moon glasses to protect your eyes. I made them just for this, please put them on." The audience put them on and behold the moon was there, right before their eyes. "Please don't take your glasses off; you may be blinded for a while if you do." She waited for the applause, but there was nothing but silence. "Do you have any questions about my power? About who I am?" She waited for them to ask how she did it, but no one asked...

She thought about the miracles of the greatest book ever written. She thought about how His miracles were not enough. *Even then they sought to kill him, and for me they still want my beauty. That is all they want.* She waved her hand back and the ceiling closed up. "You can take your glasses off! Tonight the moon is before your eyes."

Blaine got up and started to clap his hands… "Bravo", he yelled, "Bravo!" He was just about to ask her secret when someone from the audience yelled out, "It was because of the glasses!" Another one screamed, "You said you had a better trick other than you, but your beauty is the greatest trick of all…" "How much, how much for you?!", "Yes", they all began to say, "How much for you?" She knew there was danger because it was her last act…

Tears came down from her eyes, "I knew you beasts would say this… I knew you would think it was the glasses, but remember I said it would be touching the cross by the old abandoned Church… The final act is waiting for you all outside." Blaine got up with excitement and disgust at the audience's behavior. "I can't wait to see the cross and the moon…" When he got outside he was beyond words and couldn't even believe what he was seeing… "My God, look what she has done. I feel like heaven has touched the earth, how does she do this, where does this magic come from?" He ran back into the theater. "Come and see what she has done." But it was noisy with men and woman yelling… "Where has she gone? Where is that deceiver! We want her, just her beauty that's all we ever asked for!" the Audience screamed… But she had disappeared, and was nowhere to be found…

The fateful night had turned into day. Days had turned into weeks, weeks into months, and still no sign of Auralia.

Blaine felt desperate and hoped to God she was safe. And so he spent every day traveling far and wide searching for his enchantress.

He immediately regretted going outside to see her last illusion. Seeing the moon touch the church steeple was nothing short of a miracle and certainly a once in a lifetime chance. However, in experiencing that chance he had missed out on a greater one. The chance to finally meet her. If he had just stayed inside he could have comforted her and then maybe she would not have disappeared.

While pondering his last memory of her, he spoke into the air on the dusty highway, "Can I get your autograph on this lonely road?"

There was no answer.

Auralia was gone without a trace. Only the memory of her lingered. Like her magic, invisible yet tangible.

Before she had disappeared, she had written a note. It was addressed to no one. And yet, it was clearly directed at everyone. Her fans, the hordes of devoted followers left longing for her beauty:

"I have surprised the world with my magic, but my magic has been my only company...Every man who has said they loved me, loved me only for my secrets, my powers, but most of all for my beauty. No one sees the real me. They do not see my soul. None have seen me. None, and so I must disappear..."

Auralia vanished like clouds over the moon, like mist across a river, like daylight when night appears...

She was gone; no one had seen her since her last performance. She had not known her secret admirer existed. She had not realized her dreams had been so close.

Blaine had also written a poem. Not with a pen and paper, but on his heart.

Disappeared
Act I

I remember your last show, I was there
You know I love you...You know I care
I was too quiet like a prayer
Your kiss I wanted to share
But do I dare or just stare...
Your eyes hypnotized me
You made my heart feel free
Now you are gone and it feels like death
I wanted to kiss you and feel your breath
You just disappeared
I needed more time
I even bought your favorite wine
Please, I love you
Please, come back
Please...
I am lost and lonely
You are the one and only
Confused and unclear
And you disappeared
God I feel so cold
My magic, my gold
Reappear to me
So I can love thee
Reappear to me

Blaine, a tortured artist, was dying inside. He knew Auralia was the love of his life. Her soul spoke the language only his understood. Time had passed but his feelings for her did not fade. His search was tireless, even going so far as to search out other illusionists who could teach him how she had used her magic to disappear. Even the best illusionists had no answers to give.

No one knew where she lived. She was a gypsy spirit. Some didn't even think she had a home. There was only one place left he had not checked out. Spirit Lake Idaho, a small town she had performed in years previously. When he arrived he was greeted by an old man. He believed she could be found in a cabin deep in the woods near Mirror Lake. The old man demanded to know who he was searching for the beautiful illusionist.

"I am her secret admirer, I have searched for years looking for her so I can finally be with her. I have always wanted to tell her I loved her, but I never did."

"Why...Why...WHY did you not tell her?" the old man stuttered in exasperation.

"I was intimidated by her beauty, I did not feel rich or handsome enough to tell her how I felt," Blaine hung his head low ashamed of his cowardice words.

"That is a damn shame. She always wanted to be loved for who she was. I would have loved her, but I am too old now. Young man, it does not matter what you look like, besides you are a fine looking gentleman. But you can never be a coward and expect to find the woman of your dreams."

"How dare you call me a coward Sir!" But Blaine knew it was true.

"No wonder why she disappeared. In Idaho we are hunters and men of wolves, not cowards...If you find her, tell her you want and love her and never let her disappear again." And with that the old man turned and walked away.

Tell Her

Act II
A Secret Admirer just will not do
If I find you I will tell you
I will tell you of how you made me feel
how you made my soul real
I want to talk to you about mysteries
I want to disappear into your mystery
I do not have much, but I will be your man
Like gone with the wind I just do not give a damn
I should have never let you go
I watched you vanish at your show
A thousand times I wanted to tell you
A thousand times I did nothing
Lucky I heard you still have not found a lover
I hope one day to be your man under the cover
Hope Fully you are somewhere down by Mirror Lake
I hope...I hope...For true love's sake!

Blaine went to Mirror Lake, but he did not find her...He went to another Idaho town called Bottle Bay. She was not there either. The only comfort to be found was in the blueberry pancakes and the view from the resort's window. For the beauty reminded him of Auralia.

As he daydreamed and stared off in the distance an older woman interrupted his thoughts, "Have you tried Green Bay?" How did she know he was looking for someone? As if a mind reader the lady spoke again, "You have been talking out loud to yourself for the past hour, repeating over and over, how do you find the Illusionist?"
"How do I get there?" He ignored the fact that he must look insane. "Oh you have to go through the dark forest just south of here. It's a big beach full of skipping stones, more stones than you will ever see. You'll find her there!" She said insistently.

"How do you know Auralia is there?" Blaine could not believe it.
"I just know. Now go tell her what you need to tell her. But I must warn you, it will be a dark trail for you, a forbidden road..." She trailed off as if she was about to fade away herself.

"I will take my car, I will get there quickly." Nothing will keep me from her now, Blaine thought
.
The woman quietly and forebodingly whispered, "Oh no young man, you have to walk to where she is. She is at the end of a dark trail. I have a map for you and I have kept her last letter for this very moment. For you. Now go!

**Auralia's Letter
No Longer Beautiful**

Act III
I will no longer be beautiful for this world
I will just be me, this normal girl
I will no longer wear make-up
I will no longer play dress up
I will just be me, this normal girl
Do not send me flowers to get me in bed
Just send me love and love me instead
Do not give me a diamond ring
Then wish for the other thing
No more bad boys, no more devil's horns
I will be like the wind and be reborn
Stop drooling with your sexy spit
Stop promising love and not giving me it
I just want to hide in these woods and be alone
No more drunks and evil thrones
I will no longer be beautiful for this world
Unless you are the one
Unless you are magic from above
I do not want another knight in shining armor, but a man of real love
No more vampire bats, give me one handsome dove
For how can a woman truly be beautiful
Unless she is truly loved...

With map and letter in hand, Blaine followed the trail, into the dark, into the woods and called out for her...
Are You Here?

Act IV
Are you here
The woman with beautiful tears
The lady who can disappear
The woman I have always wanted
Come, do not be daunted
Come, I am the one that is haunted
By your soul, your pale light
Like moonlight...
Why are you here hiding in these dark woods
you are the only thing I know that is good
Come please and ask me my name
I want true love and to feel no shame
Not for wanting you
Like a white flower wanting the color blue
I am here, I am waiting for you...

A strange noise and an eerie feeling came over him. Blaine thought, "What was that? Is that her, is she here?" The strange noise changed now and was getting closer. It was footsteps he heard now.

It had happened. Blaine and Auralia had finally come face to face, as fate had preordained.

"Is that you, are you here?" Blaine said.
"Yes I am here, but I am not the same." she said quietly.
"Come out and let me see you please," he whispered back.

"You do not want to see me. Shadows have become my blankets of comfort. I am better off here, than out there with you."

"What has happened to you?" Blaine couldn't believe what he was hearing.

"Do you see that tree with the rope hanging from it?" she said with a trembling voice.

"Yes, yes I do..." he wished he could only hold her.

"That was me."

"How is that you?" he said, so confused.

"That is where I hung myself. There was no early magic, I disappeared by killing myself." Auralia's voice was trembling now.

"But you are here, speaking with me now..."

"I am only partly here; the rest of me is dead." she said and stepped closer to Blaine. All he could see was her chest, the rest was still in the shadows.

Blaine immediately noticed a scar running down the middle of her chest, "Who did this to you?"
"This was what I have to show for my first attempt. My second time was done in the Tree of Death, but it was not me. I did not do it..." she said.
"A second time? Then how are you here?" he questioned.
"I was dead for 3 days. I did not die in glory, but I did wake in glory."
"Is there someone you love?" Blaine had to know.
"Not that kind of love, another kind of love, there is 4 kinds of love you know. Words, we live in words, it is how the world began. With spoken words..." she said.
"What kind of words?" he asked.
"Heaven is made up of such words upon words. Every word said there takes action, not like here where words are wind in the air...It was everything you could ever imagine, and of course it is where imagination has always been." her words were like oxygen to him, he needed her words like lungs need air. He understood her meaning perfectly..

"You mean imagination was never born nor created."

"Yes, precisely!" she was pleased.

"Why do you still have a scar on your chest if heaven is where you were?" he asked.

"Oh you do not know? The only earthly thing made in heaven is scars."

"What is the difference then? We can use our imagination here on earth?" he had so many questions for her.

"Our words here come from a dying kiss. In heaven the mystery is there is no flesh and blood. There is light, but not the same kind of light as we have here. It is a place where there is no darkness, not like the darkness of the universe."

"I have heard that light needs darkness." Blaine said. "Oh no! Not this kind of light, not the light of soul, love and imagination.

Believe me, heaven is not a boring place. It is everything good you have ever imagined, and more." and with that Auralia stepped back into the darkness.

Blaine asked Auralia why she had come back. "And I heard those that kill themselves end up in hell."
"Let us say that suicide is not a pretty ending, and not glorifying."
What would be next for them now that he had found her and there was nothing to be done. Auralia just then walked out from the shadows to show herself completely. Blaine immediately saw that she was nothing like herself.

Auralia then spoke "Men have only ever loved me for my beauty and never for who I really was. So I took my own life, but my life was not mine to take. I understand that now. When heaven came I was shown all the different roads I could have taken. I saw you in the reflection of the water of heaven and you were looking for me. I heard the things you thought about me. I read your poems written for me. I begged God, 'Please, I did not know there was such a man that existed who loves me!' God then told me, 'Never take or destroy your life because of how the world sees you. NEVER GIVE PEOPLE THE POWER TO DESTROY WHAT YOU ARE!' Then he asked softly, 'Do you really think he loves you?'

"I do, even if I was not pretty, I believe he would still love me.

The Almighty continued, "You know that I know, but it is you that needs to know."

"Just tell me." Auralia said.

He responded, "I am much more trusted when my words come to life and are lived, not just told. I will send you back without your beauty so you can find out if he really loves you, then you will know for certain."

Auralia said in a foreboding tone, "God also said that this would not be a good ending. And that was part of the test. He wanted me to tell you that either way the ending is not good. So I walk back into the forest and you have three days to decide what to do, but before I go I will take one more step out from the darkness so you can really see all of me."

As she stepped out, he grew sad for she looked frail and wasted. Her once peach pale skin was now saggy worn gray, a hideous phantom with no beauty to entertain his eyes. He wanted to shut his eyes from the sight but he refrained from doing so to avoid hurting her further.
"If you still love me you must now come into the shadows and find me. But I must warn you, in here you will find the creature of death, and it will end badly either way as God has said." And with that said Auralia disappeared again.

Blaine felt the weight of the world on his shoulders. Everything he had ever wanted seemed to be destroyed. He could not think of the phantom creature she had become. He also did not understand why God would make some things beautiful and some things ugly. "Why?!" he shouted aloud to himself. He could not fathom why life had to be so difficult and tumultuous.

On the second day Blaine thought of how both endings would be horrible. Why would God have created a life to end so horribly? But his love for Auralia was the only glimmer of hope he felt. Nothing else seemed to truly matter. Not the disfigured phantom, not the darkness of the forest, or the fear he felt for the creature of death...only his pure transcendent love for Auralia was relevant.

Even with that light feeling, he knew on the third day when he found her and kissed her, he would be kissing the lips of death.

Kiss Of Death
Act V
I will kiss her even if there is two horrible outcomes
I will kiss her even if I am not winning
I will be brave and believe
That somehow love is all we need
Even if my heart breaks and bleeds
this may be my last breath
When I kiss her it will be the kiss of death
Death has ruined everything
Cursed and is never blessed
But if I go back into the world
I would have never kissed my lovely girl
Though her beauty is gone
All beauty fades when youth is gone
Even so...I still love her so
On the third day he ran into the woods at dawn. He ran as fast as his legs could carry him. Nothing would keep him from finding her again.
Upon arriving at the spot he had found her days before he yelled at the top of his out of breath lungs, "I love you, I love you, I have always loved you and I always will!"

The Dark Tree
Act IV

As he finished proclaiming his love, he noticed that the darkness grew. The sun had been blotted out by the trees, as if they were conspiring together to close it off from him. A cold wind blew and swirled leaves around his face. And as they settled around his feet and the wind stopped he heard a terrifying voice:

"Do you love her? If you do, she is deeper within the dark forest, and you cannot outrun Him." the dark trees spoke.

"I thought trees were friendly." Blaine retorted.

"You are correct. However the death spirit is not congenial." the dark trees said, "It is the spirit of death that comes to claim us all when it is our time. He lives here and is here now, watching."

"I am not afraid." Blaine said hoping his voice would not betray his fear, "It does not matter, for both outcomes are tragic."

"Oh, but one is better than the other. Did you not know that there are two kinds of death in this life. Auralia hung herself on the death tree, but there is only one person that hung on that tree and escaped..."

Blaine demanded to know who. And the dark trees mysteriously answered with, "You will see."

He started running deeper into the woods, but the darkness was swirling around him making it nearly impossible to see where he was going. Blaine had no idea if he was even running in the right direction, let alone if he were ever going to find his way back out again. He was all in now, whether he wanted it or not.

Breathlessly Blaine called out, "I am here! Come out Auralia!"

"Climb to the top of the rocks just up the hill, then look down into the darkest part of the clearing, you will see me." she called out.
"There you are," Blaine said, "Let us go, I am getting out of this place."

But Auralia had other plans, "The dark trees were right you know...would you still love me if you knew who I really was? Never tell my secrets? Can you truly love a woman that wars with herself every day...
Loves every night
A thousand poems written in fire and cold
A thousand more to be written of how much I love you
Your soft hands of poetry and hard hands of love, pain, and regret
Dripping with ink blood down the pages of this haunted life
What would you do Blaine?
Where would you go?
Forget this world
There is a new story to be written
Where love never dies
Just come with me now
And vanish
Vanish with me

"Of course Auralia, it is all I have ever wanted, and needed." Blaine said.

"Then RUN, we have to run before we are hung from the tree."

As she spoke that cold wind began again and the wind blew between the trees, causing the great dark trees to creak and moan. She could hear the death spirit crawling closer and closer.

"How is it that I can see this different form of darkness behind us? It is not like the kind of darkness caused from a lack of light." Blaine wondered.

"The Death Spirit is an unnatural darkness; It is like a backwards, inside out light...and if we do not run to the natural light, we will be dead for certain. But if truth be told, only one person has ever outrun the dark spirit of death...only one person has hung on the tree of death, and lived on. If we do not outrun this darkness, it will hang us here in these trees for eternity," she said with fear in her voice.

"I understand now. That is the one tragic ending. What is the other?" he asked.
"That is up to you Blaine. It is something only you can see and understand for yourself."

They continued running hand in hand through the forest while the wind blew fiercely. There was no daylight to be seen and the darkness behind seemed to be gaining. Hope was fading fast.

"I grow weary of running. I am tired of being afraid and I am tired of not living my belief. Who is this person that has escaped the death spirit? How can we find him? Before you answer there is one thing I must do." Blaine then gently placed his hands on her phantom face, and leaned in slowly, placing his warm mouth upon her pale red lips. For a second there was no darkness surrounding them. For a moment eternity was there, found within that transcending kiss of love.

Then his hands began to tremble and the unnatural darkness consumed them both. "What is happening?" Blaine called out.

He looked into her eyes and saw she was fading from his sight. He looked down to see his own fingers crumbling away like dusty mud in the wind that would not stop.

"You knew I would be the kiss of death Blaine. I am not alive. Before this death encircled us completely, we must continue to the light and face the third and final death." Auralia said.

"What? You told me there was only two horrible endings..." he said.

"That is true, but I have no time to explain it now, you must run. Run NOW!" she cried out.

They took off with a newfound hope. They could see light up ahead for the first time. The dark wind behind them grew stronger, angrier. Trees were falling like a tornado of evil uprooting them.

They emerged free from the woods, up to the edge of the light. It was like arms lifting them into the air, a triumphant feeling of victory, an eruption of rapturous relief beaming straight into their souls.

Blaine looked over at Auralia and saw her beauty restored and the smile on her face was once again the miracle he had hoped for.

"Oh my love, your beauty has come back, and you are more beautiful than ever. Look a river, a wonderful sparkling river is here and I am so thirsty. Come let us drink my love, we did it. I'm so happy, look my fingers are not crumbling away as dust, they're shining like brilliant diamonds." he said.

As Blaine bent over to drink, he saw their images in the river. There they were in the dark woods, hanging lifeless from the tree.

"I don't understand..." he said.

The audience stopped looking at him and turned their faces towards her. *"She's beautiful, more beautiful than the moon in the sky."* With softened hearts; they craved to hear her reply. The essence of her words finally was understood and matched her beauty... They hadn't seen the complete beauty of who she was. The phantom she once was, they now understood in their own shallowness.

The audience strained to hear her words.
A cough broke the silence. Brushing back her long hair and looking into Blaine's eyes knowing he knew it all along; she tuned to the audience and said,

"This is the End of Illusion."

END OF ILLUSION

Take a Glimpse of the Novel Secret of the Blood

Chapter Trailers

Green Eyes on Ice~ Lucian, a young man from NYC moves to the inland Pacific Northwest for reasons unknown. Through his exceptional physical feats and dark poetry he establishes himself as a local legend. There are many questions and a dark mystique surrounding his association with Foreverlightless, a NYC goth nightclub. An obsession with immortality permeates Lucian's poetry and his very being. During a brush with death Lucian finds the love he's been searching for in Kael, a green-eyed beauty with whom Lucian shares the secrets of Foreverlightless. His wish for Kael to join him in his quest for immortality is seemingly cut short by tragedy on an icy moonlit night.

High Mass~ *Four months earlier* Delila, a young gothic beauty finds herself attending a midnight mass at St. Patrick's Cathedral in NYC. The ceremony is interrupted by a psychopathic character who physically and verbally attacks and denigrates the very acts and ideas of religious ceremony and rite. Identifying himself as Lucian, he proclaims the advent of a new way replacing the old.

Blink 69~ *The next day* finds friends Delila and Lisa on a train heading upstate to attend a football game. Missing the previous night's drama, Lisa plies Delila with questions about Lucian. Lisa and Lucian have established a puzzling yet smoldering romance based primarily on the club action of Foreverlightless and Lucian's poetry. Lucian is on the same train. As a walk-on player he has wowed everyone, including pro scouts with his on-field feats that seem super-human.

Strawberry Blink~ Lisa confronts Lucian on the train trying to figure out where things stand with their relationship. Lucian hints at things to come and offers a token of his intentions albeit still vague and poetic.

Pearl Blink~ Lisa and Delila ponder and discuss Lucian's gift. The jewelry he's given Lisa not only accelerates and elevates the relationship, it grants exclusive access and privilege to the extreme side of Foreverlightless which is where Lucian thrives.

Lisa ponders an earlier encounter with Lucian with her father that still haunts her. Choices need to be made and it seems Lucian's spell is drawing Lisa deeper into whatever it is he is involved with. Lisa is still unsure of just what it is but relishes the goth club scene and the obvious physical attraction she has for Lucian.

Hail Mary, Blink Right~ It's game time and everyone's there except Lucian. Accosted and beaten savagely by members of the rival football team who have gotten word of Lucian's antics at the cathedral and his goth ways, Lucian is bound and imprisoned. Miraculously, Lucian appears late in the game, unscathed and ready to wreak havoc on the field. It's the Lucian Show. It appears that Lucian's actions, especially these last 2 days have been carefully scripted and planned to propagate and establish his legacy. He has become the poster-boy/ambassador for Foreverlightless. Within the course of a few football plays, Lucian single-handedly destroys the rival team/captors, and seemingly wins the game. The superhuman physicality that Lucian displays, witnessed by Lisa and others more than hints at his involvement with some extraordinary power or process.

Lloyd's Surprise~ A pre-arranged romantic rendezvous following Lucian's epic display leaves Lisa shaken after she experiences a dark, sinister presence she can't explain.

A Rose is a Rose is a Rose~ While making his way with Lisa to catch the train home Lucian again demonstrates his intentions with a reference to an Oscar Wilde poem that will become central to Lucian's theology. Comical, extreme irony abounds as they race to catch their ride home.

Bannerman's Blink~ Lucian's extravagantly scripted train-ride home leaves Lisa breathless despite the brief recurrence of the ominous, dark presence. Displaying the power and influence of Foreverlightless, Lucian passionately implores Lisa to join him in his quest for immortality. Scoffing at the world's view of vampires and related subject matter he proclaims himself as already having unlocked the secrets of immortality through genetic engineering, virtual reality, blood rejuvenation and more. "Foreverlightless provides the science, research and financial resources, I provide the theology."

Lucian makes one last grand display as he leaves Lisa when she is unable to totally commit to his offer. Before leaving for the Pacific Northwest where our story began, Lucian leaves a cryptic note that only later Lisa understands.

Pascal and Elymas /Morning After Pearl ~

July 12 ~ July13, 2014, Nine months later in Rome, Italy Dr. Pascal, a world-renowned psychologist/criminal profiler finds himself returning to the castle of an illusionist that he has been obsessed with for years. He would trade all he has to uncover the secret behind the grand illusion Elymas has been astounding the world with for years. Finding himself the primary participant in Elymas' grand finale, Pascal is convinced to take Elymas as a patient to try and uncover and analyze the dark premonitions of blood and death plaguing the magician. What will comes from this twisted alliance? Are these premonitions linked to reality? What's with the pearls and hummingbirds?

Preflight~ *July 18, 2014* Nine months have passed since Lucian left Lisa at Bannerman's Castle. Lisa has spent that time enjoying the exclusive access to Foreverlightless that Lucian had bestowed on her. The combination of virtual reality and bloodmagicstir potions has Lisa addicted to the darker side of the dance club that few know about. Sporadic and limited contact with Lucian through virtual reality leaves Lisa clueless about their relationship but club life more than offsets any negatives.

   Lucian finally contacts Lisa this night and they share a passionate virtual reality experience culminating in an invitation for Lisa and her friends to join him in the Pacific Northwest.

Night Flight~ *July 19* The very next night finds Lisa and her friends in Coeur d'Alene, Idaho at Lazzaretto House, an extension of Foreverlightless that has a heritage steeped in gothic history. Lucian swoops in for Lisa and they fly off to his "castle" on Lake Pend Oreille 30 minutes north. Lucian exerts more pressure on Lisa to join him in his quest that is finally taking shape in Lisa's mind. Later in the story exactly what lays behind the stone cliffs is discovered. This discovery by an unlikely source will only add fuel to the approaching firestorm that will engulf our characters in a couple of days.

L&L Fly~ *July 21* Whatever took place at Lucian's castle has led to this special night that Lucian has dreamed of... a consummation, a wedding of sorts. The glamour and technology of Foreverlightless is now forefront and becoming more apparent to Lisa as Lucian pledges his life to her atop NYC. Probing the limits of romance, Lucian pushes the limits of sacrifice and commitment as their free-flight through the city ends in a gripping watery finale that will turn this story on its head.

Is Lucian, the dark poet a narcissistic raving lunatic with delusions of grandeur? Have the experiments, training and genetic manipulation broken Lucian? Find out why the first chapter of this story is written in a different font. What of Lisa? Is there a malignant evil behind the secret doors of Foreverlightless? What is this power seeking to consume all who succumb to this gothic psycho-sensual lure?

NSTAV~ *July 22* It now appears that a serial killer is to blame for three deaths within the last 2 weeks. Detective Willard wasn't sure until now. This latest body in Central park confirms it. There seems a connection to Foreverlightless that prompts the news media to label these murders "Death of Twilight" killings due to the vampiric nature of Foreverlightless and the goth lifestyle of the victims.

Near the breaking point due to the recent death of his wife, Willard struggles to maintain his sanity. A mysterious phone call interrupts his investigation in Central Park and he finds himself alone with another body and the possible killer in the Tattooed Forest of Foreverlightless. It appears the victim Willard finds is__

Whiskey and Waffles~ *July 22-23, Tues/Wed*
Overwhelmed by the presence and specter of death, Willard seeks to diminish his responsibilities in the case by convincing his superior to call in an expert in this field. Recruiting this experts' assistance is anything but routine considering the history shared with Willard.

This bizarre reunion of ex-partners is accented by an unnerving discovery as Willard knocks on Van Bibber's front door. When chilling details beyond the realm of coincidence are laid out stark and bare by Willard, VB, who is battling personal problems of his own joins the investigation.

Foreverlightless~ *July 24, Thursday* Back in the city he abandoned three years prior, VB immediately follows up on the data Willard had given him. Cult crimes were VB's specialty. As a P.I. he has established himself as the best. "Van Helsing...Van Bibber... they'll both get the job done."

Haunted by reminders of the serial killer case that nearly cost him his life, VB struggles to rebuild his life with Kelly his wife and Johnny Walker Red, no ice. Things currently aren't going so well. Denied access to Foreverlightless, VB goes native and infiltrates the scene, embarking on a midnight foray deep into the far reaches of the Foreverlightless compound.

The Tattooed Forest~ VB penetrates the outer defenses of the Foreverlightless grounds and finds himself surround by the carvings on the trees in the Tattooed Forest. Cryptic poems and messages hundreds of years old with famous and anonymous signatures to be believed or not stare VB in the face. The legacy of Foreverlightless, just as rumors belied, run deep and strong with strong hints of vampirism and cultic practice. Carvings by Lisa and Lucian along with those from the very hand of Oscar Wilde particularly catch VB's eye along with other names that will surely figure in the grand scheme of the case. VB is interrupted by what appears to be a crime in progress only to discover that he is witnessing a sensual, ritualistic game of hide and seek. VB finds the spot where Willard discovered the body and makes the biggest discovery in the case so far.

Dark Wishing Well~ VB comes upon a sort of vampire funeral at the site of what turns out to be a technological marvel. VB confronts the mysterious character Stonelight who immediately inserts himself into the muddled mix of players in the case. A puzzling brief encounter with Lucian only adds to VB's confusion as he attempts to sort through the facts and clues.

Foreverlightless Harbor~ Witnessing a seaside séance, VB now knows that this case is unlike any other he has ever been involved with. He questions a frightened, delusional Delila who hints at a force responsible for the deaths of her friends. All the secrets and clues seem to lie deep behind the doors of Foreverlightless. Returning empty-handed to his motel VB ruminates on the case and his life in general. An early morning call from Willard has him on a direct flight when more bodies are discovered in The Pacific Northwest.

Need maginfy glass to read the blood map

Blood Map

Investigating the crime scene, I could never imagine that I would be investigating a blood story that would lead me here...

My partner's wife died of a rare blood disease... I found bodies hanging in trees with vampire marks on their necks and no blood to be found.

I've been to the mountains of Yukon drinking scotch while an old man drank wild lamb blood and told me tales of bloodless angels. That day in the mountain, in the cave, Stonelight showed me pictures of ancient blood sacrifices thousands of years old.

My investigation has led me to the underground club called "Forever Lightless" in Manhattan and all the way to the woods of North Idaho to some North Idaho College students in Coeur d'Alene.

All this, searching for my main suspect, the dark poet who wrote a poetry book called "Blood Magic Stir" after the disappearance of his lover Kael.

Yesterday in my hotel, smoking my last cigarette, I read about an unwelcomed guest at a midnight high mass where a man throws the communion cup across the church yelling, "There's no immortality in this cup."

Blood.... What is all this blood? Should I go on?

I'm now here in a forest they call, "The Tattooed Forest" where there are carvings and keep sakes in the trees. In the middle of the forest is a deep stony well they call the "Dark Wishing Well", part of another blood ritual. But this isn't ancient...this is now.

What am I searching for? What are they searching for? What are we searching for?

"The Secret of the Blood..."

Contacts

Novel

Secret of the Blood

by

Wayne Mussatto & Denny Mussatto

Websites

secretoftheblood.com
darkwishingwell.com
stonelightpublishing.com

Facebook

End of Illusion

Lucian Wilde

Secret of the Blood (Death of Twilight)

Dark Side of Genius

Poetry Tour

Dark Side of Genius by Denny Mussatto
© Stonelight Publishing

www.ingramcontent.com/pod-product-compliance
Lightning Source LLC
Chambersburg PA
CBHW022101090426
42743CB00008B/683